THE BUSH LEGACY

THEIR STORY IN PHOTOGRAPHS

Created by David Elliot Cohen

Foreword by Condoleezza Rice

Essay by Donald L. Evans

STERLING
New York

STERLING
New York

An Imprint of Sterling Publishing
387 Park Avenue South
New York, NY 10016

Library of Congress Cataloging-in-Publication Data

Cohen, David, 1955-
   The Bush legacy : their story in photographs / created by David Elliot Cohen;
foreword by Condoleeza Rice; essay by Donald Evans.
    p. cm.
    ISBN 978-1-4027-8787-4
    1. Bush family--Pictorial works.   2. Bush, Prescott Sheldon, 1895-1972--Pictorial
works.   3. Bush, George. 1924---Pictorial works.   4. Bush, George, W. (George Walker),
1946--Pictorial works.   5. Presidents--United States--Pictorial works.   I. Evans, Donald
Louis, 1946- II. Title.
    E883.B87C65 2011
    973.928092'2--dc22
                                        2011014760

Distributed in Canada by Sterling Publishing c/o Canadian Manda Group,
165 Dufferin Street, Toronto, Ontario, Canada M6K 3H6
Distributed in the United Kingdom by GMC Distribution Services
Castle Place, 166 High Street, Lewes, East Sussex, England BN7 1XU
Distributed in Australia by Capricorn Link (Australia) Pty. Ltd.
P.O. Box 704, Windsor, NSW 2756, Australia

Please see page 222 and 224 for text and picture credits

For information about custom editions, special sales, and premium and corporate purchases, please
contact Sterling Special Sales at 800-805-5489 or specialsales@sterlingpublishing.com.

Manufactured in China

2 4 6 8 10 9 7 5 3 1

www.sterlingpublishing.com

▶ **FUTURE PRESIDENTS:** World War II hero and Yale scholar-athlete, George H. W.
Bush holds nine-month-old George W. in New Haven, Connecticut, April 1947.

FOREWORD

By Condoleezza Rice

Professor of political economy, Stanford Graduate School of Business
Special Assistant to President George H. W. Bush for National Security Affairs
US National Security Advisor to President George W. Bush (2001–2004)
US Secretary of State (2005–2009)

I have had the distinct privilege of working for two US presidents in my career, President George Herbert Walker Bush and President George Walker Bush, a father and a son united by shared values, deep patriotism, and unconditional love. The son of US Senator Prescott Bush, George H. W. Bush instilled in his children the notion that public service is an honorable course for one's life and worth pursuing. Indeed, three generations of Bush men, and women, have held positions of power and responsibility in Washington.

When one thinks about the impact the Bushes have had on America and the world, one must consider the enormity of the moment in which each president served, one at the end of a great historical epoch, the Cold War contest between communism and democratic capitalism, and the other at the dawn of a new epoch characterized by transnational threats and violent extremism.

◀ **THE PATRIARCH:** Prescott Sheldon Bush (1895–1972), father and grandfather of American presidents. The tall, elegant son of a Columbus, Ohio, steel magnate, "Pres" played baseball and led the glee club at Yale, saw combat as a World War I artillery captain, and secured a lucrative partnership at Brown Brothers Harriman, Wall Street's oldest, most prestigious private bank. Like his father-in-law, George Herbert Walker, he became president of the US Golf Association. An early supporter of Planned Parenthood and the United Negro College Fund, the socially liberal, fiscally conservative Bush was a rock-ribbed New England Republican who served as a US senator from Connecticut from 1952 to 1963.

I was in the White House on both 11/9, the day the Berlin Wall came down without a shot fired, and 9/11, a day of unimaginable horror. These were times that presented novel challenges and forced decisions of tremendous consequence to the international system. These were times when leadership truly mattered, not just for the United States but also for the world, and I am grateful that in each case, a President Bush occupied the Oval Office.

I was in the White House on both 11/9, the day the Berlin Wall came down without a shot fired, and 9/11, a day of unimaginable horror.... These were times when leadership truly mattered.

Both men understood well that the advance of freedom creates conditions for peace, that the United States, as a great power, ought to have a view of how human history should unfold, and that the United States must not shy away from upholding values known to be universal and true. Nevertheless, it was hard work that demanded political courage, clarity of vision, and an understanding that today's headlines and history's judgment are rarely the same.

When I served in the administration of President George H. W. Bush from 1989 to 1991 as the Soviet specialist in the National Security Council, I saw the liberation of Eastern Europe, the unification of Germany on Western terms, and the beginnings of the peaceful collapse of the Soviet Union. These were remarkable achievements, and yet President Bush was mocked in the press at the time. Today, President Bush's quiet diplomacy with Helmut Kohl and Mikhail Gorbachev is widely praised, and Europe stands whole, free, and at peace.

After the attacks of 9/11, it was clear that the United States lacked the tools to identify and confront the threats of the twenty-first century. As national security advisor to President George W. Bush, I sought to build these tools and reform our institutions to adapt to the challenges of terrorism, failed states, and the proliferation of dangerous materials around the world. In these efforts, President George W. Bush led the United States with steady resolve and compassion, keeping the homeland safe for the duration of his administration and quadrupling aid to the poorest people on the planet.

Secretary Rice and President Bush at the United Nations in September 2007.   **Photograph by Jim Watson**

I came to know the forty-first and the forty-third president of the United States as leaders on the world stage, but also as wonderful human beings, devoted to their family and kind to their friends. In the pages that follow, you will discover a moving collection of photographs that document the historic, quotidian, and raw moments of one of America's most extraordinary families. David Elliot Cohen uses his curatorial expertise to provide the reader with a transporting experience inside family gatherings and behind closed doors. You will learn of the early roots of the Bush family in Connecticut, see views of the Atlantic from Walker's Point, and attend meetings in the Oval Office. And you will come to know the Bush family, much as I have, for their decency, humility, and singularly American qualities.

Stanford, California
March 2011

HOME: In 1923, after two years of marriage, Prescott Bush of Columbus, Ohio, and his wife, the former Dorothy Walker of St. Louis, headed east. They landed at 173 Adams Street in Milton, Massachusetts, **top**, where the second of their four sons, George Herbert Walker Bush, was born on June 12, 1924. In 1925, Prescott took a job with United States Rubber (one of the twelve original Dow Jones Industrials) in New York City. The family moved to the afflu-ent New York suburb of Greenwich, Connecticut. This house on Grove Lane, **bottom**, would shelter the expanding Bush family for the next thirty years.

FIRST STEPS: George Herbert Walker Bush, just a year old, in Kennebunkport, Maine, circa 1925. The toddler was named after his maternal grandfather, George Herbert "Bert" Walker, a wealthy, larger-than-life investment banker from St. Louis. Walker was president of the US Golf Association (the famed Walker Cup is named for him), and he co-headed the syndicate that rebuilt Madison Square Garden and the Belmont Park horse-racing track.

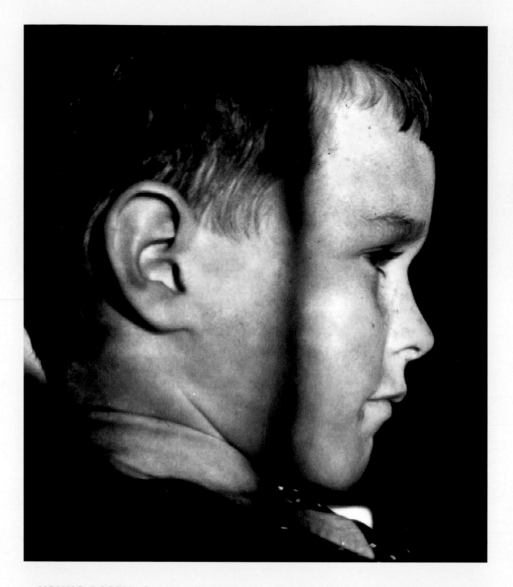

▲ **YOUNG POPPY:** George "Poppy" Bush, the second of five siblings: Prescott Jr. ("Pressy," Yale '44), George ("Poppy," Yale '48), Nancy (Vassar, '46), Jonathan ("Johnny," Yale '53), and William ("Bucky," Yale '60). George was tagged with the diminutive "Poppy" by his four young Walker uncles to distinguish the boy from his grandfather, George Herbert Walker, whom they called "Pops." The name stuck ... all the way to the White House ... though Bush never much liked it.

▶ **YOUNG BARBARA:** An early portrait of seven-year-old Barbara Bush, née Pierce—a very distant relative of the fourteenth US president, Franklin Pierce, and future wife of the forty-first president. Born in Flushing, Queens, Barbara grew up in the cozy purlieus of suburban Rye, New York. "It was a very carefree childhood," Barbara later wrote in her memoir. "One of my first memories of something really awful happening was when Charles Lindbergh's baby was kidnapped and killed in 1932"—the year this photograph was taken—"that really frightened us."

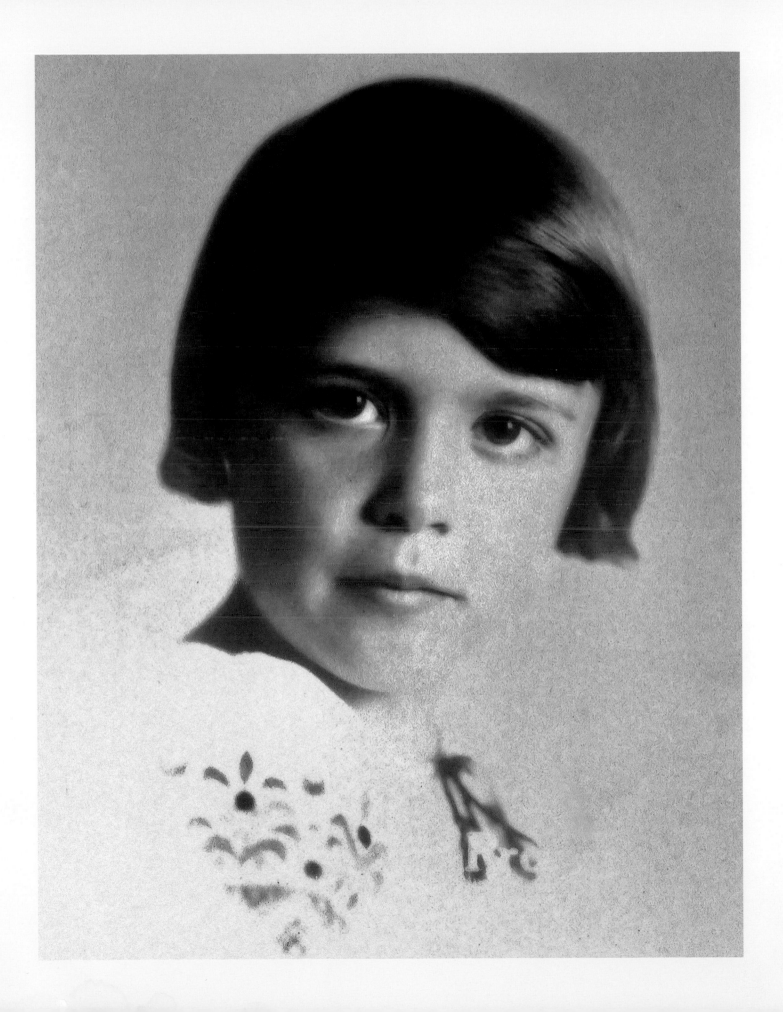

▲ **THE PIERCES OF RYE, NEW YORK:** Pauline Robinson Pierce and her four children in 1935: **l–r**, James, Scott, Barbara, and Martha. Pauline was married to Marvin Pierce, the future president of the company that published *McCall's* and *Redbook* magazines. She was a beautiful, troubled woman who lived above her means and often talked about what she would do when her "ship came in." As daughter Barbara later noted in her memoir, her mother's ship "had come in—she just didn't know it." Oldest daughter Martha, **far right**, who inherited Pauline's delicate features, was, for a while, a professional model for *Vogue* and other magazines. Barbara would opt for the domestic life—or so she thought—dropping out of Smith College at nineteen to marry a young naval aviator named Poppy Bush.

◀ **POPPY AFIELD:** In 1937, at age thirteen, Poppy Bush departed leafy Greenwich, Connecticut, to join his older brother, Pressy, at Phillips Academy (also known as Andover, to distinguish it from rival Phillips Exeter Academy in New Hampshire). The elite and, at the time, all-male Massachusetts boarding school historically prepared students for Yale. Andover's seal, designed by Paul Revere, incorporates two Latin mottos that would inform Bush's life: *Non Sibi* and *Finis Origine Pendet* ("Not for Oneself" and "The End Depends upon the Beginning").

NATURAL LEADER: At Andover, Poppy Bush quickly blossomed into a popular, well-rounded boy and a natural leader. By senior year he was class president, editorial board member of the school newspaper, captain of the baseball and soccer teams, and chairman of the annual campus charity drive. The same year, Poppy nearly died from a staph infection in his right arm, requiring a lengthy hospital stay. **At left**, Poppy performs in a school skit. **Above**, Bush plays first base for the Big Blue baseball squad.

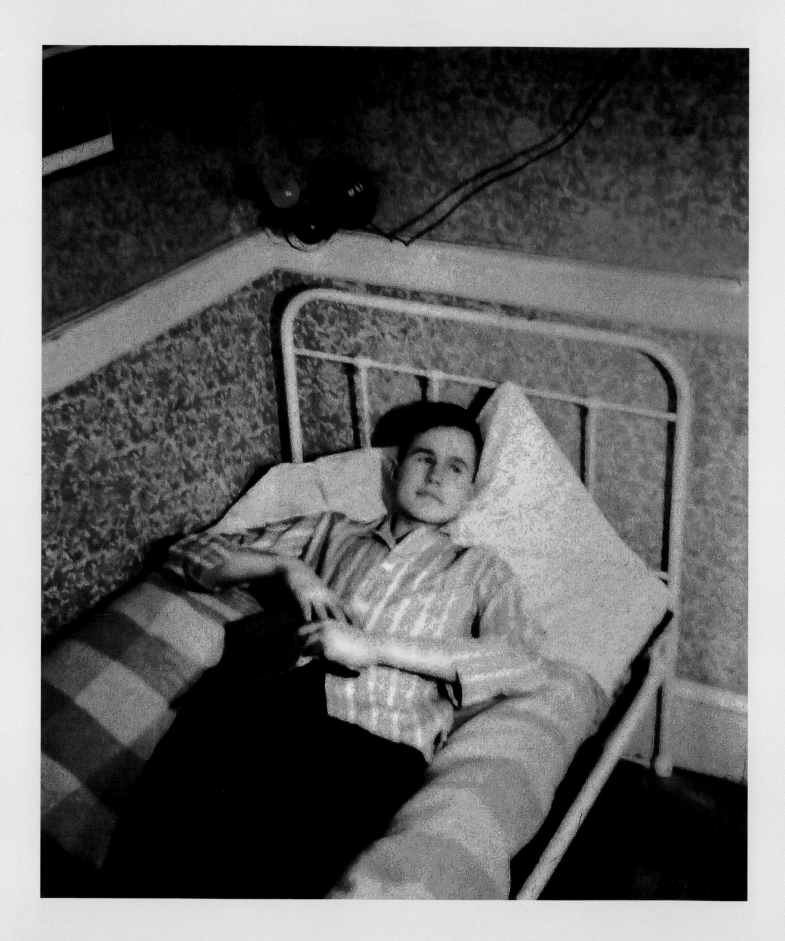

YOUNG LOVE: In December of Bush's senior year at Andover, the Japanese attacked Pearl Harbor. At Christmas break, he attended a holiday dance in Greenwich and met pretty sixteen-year-old Barbara Pierce, home for Christmas from her Charleston, South Carolina, boarding school, Ashley Hall. That night, Barbara went home and told her mother that she met "the nicest, cutest boy named Poppy." They met again the following night at another dance in Rye, and after a flurry of letters, Poppy invited Barbara to Andover's senior prom. That night, he kissed her on the cheek, and they became an item. On June 12, 1942, on his eighteenth birthday and only a few days after graduation, Bush traveled to Boston and joined the Navy. He wanted to be a naval aviator. Barbara would become the girl back home, and George would name his planes for her. **At left**, Bush relaxes in his Andover dorm room. **Above left**, Bush in his Andover soccer uniform. **Above right**, Barbara Pierce, probably the summer before she met her future husband.

NAVAL AVIATOR: Poppy Bush reported for duty at a Navy pre-flight training center in North Carolina in August 1942. The men in his unit were "a darn good-hearted bunch, so many different types of fellows!" the cadet wrote to his parents. Bush earned his wings and was commissioned at Corpus Christi Naval Air Station in Texas in June 1943, three days shy of his nineteenth birthday. At the time, he was the youngest pilot in the US Navy. **At left**, Bush in dress whites, early 1943. **Above left**, in the cockpit of a TBM Avenger torpedo bomber named *Barbara*. **Above right**, Lieutenant Junior Grade Bush with two crewmen on the flight deck of the carrier USS *San Jacinto*, circa 1944.

NAVPERS-134 (REV. 1-44)

DECK LOG—REMARKS SHEET

UNITED STATES SHIP _____ SAN JACINTO _____   SATURDAY 2 SEPTEMBER 19 44
(Day)   (Date)   (Month)

0-4 Steaming as before on base course 270°T and pgc, zigzagging according to plan #6, speed 18 knots, 183 R.P.M., standard speed 15 knots. In company with T.G. 38.4, SAN JACINTO designated as formation guide, steaming in the vicinity of the Bonin Islands. Task Group in formation 5 Roger with fleet axis on 060°T and pgc. Boilers #1 and #3 and generators #1 and #3 in use. Ship in Material Condition Baker and readiness condition #23. 0000 Ceased zigzagging and steadied on base course 0003, C/C to 250°T and pgc. 0013 Resumed zigzagging according to plan #6. 0256 Blew tubes on Boilers #1 and #3. 0303 Lighted off Boilers #2 and #4. 0355 Cut in Boilers #2 and #4.

HARLOW O. PANHORST
Lieut. Comdr., U.S.N.R.

4-8 Steaming as before. 0420 Ceased zigzagging, steadied on course 279°T. 0425 Changed course to 050°T, speed to 24 knots, 244 R.P.M., for flight operations. 0427 Sounded General Quarters. 0430-0556 Launched 18 VF and 4 VT aircraft. 0448 F6F plane #12(Bu No. 41359), piloted by Lt. J.R. MARTELLE, USNR, crashed into sea after developing engine trouble shortly after launching. Position Latitude 26°02' N, Longitude 141°33' 30"E. 0458 Pilot Lt. J. R. MARTELLE, USNR, rescued uninjured by U.S.S. McCALL(DD400). 0500 Task Unit 38.4.2 departed from formation for bombardment assignment. 0502 Changed course to 160°T, speed to 18 knots, 180 R.P.M. 0505 Changed speed to 15 knots, 150 R.P.M. 0507 Commenced zigzagging according to plan #6 on base course 160°T. 0514 Secured from General Quarters, set condition 23. 0520 Changed speed to 18 knots, 180 R.P.M. 0608 Ceased zigzagging, steadied on course 140°T. 0612 Changed course to 045°T. 0621 Commenced zigzagging on base course 045°T. 0631 ceased zigzagging, steadied on course 040°T. 0632 Kita Iwo Jima Island sighted bearing 220°T, distance 34 miles. 0636 Changed speed to 23 knots, 234 R.P.M. 0637 Changed course to 060°T. 0645 Sounded flight quarters. 0649 Changed course to 250°T, speed to 18 knots, 180 R.P.M. 0700 Mustered crew on stations. No absentees. 0712 Changed course to 060°T, speed to 22 knots, 222 R.P.M., for flight operations. 0716-0722 Launched 4 VT and 4 VF aircraft. 0723-1728 Recovered 4 VT and 3 VF aircraft. 0729 While attempting to land, F6F #22(Bu No. 42535), piloted by Lt.(jg), JULIAN MURPHY, crashed on deck at #8 sponson. No injuries to personnel. Heavy damage to plane, #8 gun mount and rails along catwalk. 0730 Changed speed to 18 knots, 180 R.P.M. 0740 Changed course to 050°T. 0750 F6F #22 jettisoned to clear deck for further operations (position Lat. 25°54'N, Long. 141°52'E). 0752 Changed speed to 19 knots, 192 R.P.M. 0752-0754 Launched 3 VF aircraft. 0754-0802 Recovered 12 VF aircraft.

JOSEPH L. SHAPIRO
Lieut. Comdr., U.S.N.R.

8-12 Steaming as before. 0803 C/S to 23 knots, 234 R.P.M. 0813 Launched 1 F6F. 0815 C/C to 190°T and pgc and C/S to 15 knots, 150 R.P.M. 0825 U.S.S. McCALL came alongside to return Lieut. J.R. MARTELLE. 0830 U.S.S. McCALL cast off. 0907 C/S to 23 knots, 234 R.P.M. 0915 C/C to 055°T and pgc. 0917-0921 Launched 4 F6F's. 0922 C/C to 240°T and pgc. 0943 C/C to 055°T and pgc. 0947-0953 Launched 4 TBM's and 8 F6F's. 0955-1003 Recovered 8 F6F's and 3 TBM's - one TBM Bu No. 46214, having crashed into sea 9 miles NE of the southern tip of Chichi Jima due to enemy anti-aircraft fire. Pilot, Lieut. (jg), G.H.W. BUSH, USNR, was rescued by submarine, but crew composed of Lt.(jg), W.G. WHITE, USNR and DELANEY, J.L., ARM2c, USN, are believed to be missing in action. 1005 Made daily inspection of magazines and smokeless powder samples - conditions normal. 1010 C/S to 21 knots, 214 R.P.M. 1040 C/C to 190°T and pgc. 1107 C/C to 210°T and pgc. 1141 C/C to 050°T and pgc and C/S to 22 knots, 224 R.P.M. 1149 C/C to 215°T and pgc.

H. L. BLUM
Lieut., U.S.N.R.

12-16 Steaming as before. 1211 Changed course to 045°T. 1214-1220 Launched 3 VT and 7 VF. 1218 Let fires die under Boilers #2 and #4. 1222-1230 Recovered 4 VT and 8 VF. 1224 Secured Boilers #2 and #4. 1230 Changed speed to 20 knots. 1238-1241 Recovered 4 VF. 1253 Launched 1 VF. 1304 Changed course to 150°T. 1313 Set condition 13. 1347 Flight quarters. 1406 Changed course to 050°T, changed speed to 22 knots. 1408-1414 Launched 10 VF. 1416-1416 Recovered 3 VT and 8 VF. 1435 Launched 2 VF. 1453 Changed course to 210°T, changed speed to 18 knots. 1456 Set condition 13. 1502 Commenced zigzagging in accordance with plan #6 on base course 210°T. 1555 Ceased zigzag, steadied on course 230°T.

F. FEUILLE
Lieut., U.S.N.R.

16-18 Steaming as before. 1602 Changed course to 050°T and pgc, changed speed to 22 knots, 224 R.P.M. 1632 Changed course to 230°T and pgc. 1645 Sounded flight quarters. 1652 Changed speed to 15 knots, 153 R.P.M. 1727 Changed course to 055°T and pgc, changed speed to 22 knots, 224 R.P.M. 1730-1739 Recovered 12 F6F's. 1745 Changed course to 175°T and pgc, changed speed to 20 knots, 203 R.P.M. 1749 Sounded General Quarters.

R. M. JOY
Lieut., U.S.N.R.

APPROVED:

H. M. MARTIN   U.S.N   COMMANDING

EXAMINED:

G. M. WINNE   U.S.N.   NAVIGATOR

TO BE FORWARDED DIRECT TO THE BUREAU OF NAVAL PERSONNEL AT THE END OF EACH MONTH
U.S. GOVERNMENT PRINTING OFFICE: 1944 O - 571992

WAR HERO: In 1944, the Allies were island-hopping across the Pacific, methodically shrinking the watery Japanese empire. During a September 2 bombing raid on the island of Chichi Jima, 600 miles south of Tokyo, Lieutenant George Bush's torpedo bomber was hit by Japanese antiaircraft fire and went down. Bush ejected and swam to his life raft, then desperately tried to keep the raft from drifting toward the Japanese-held island. The submarine USS *Finback*, on rescue patrol, picked him up. His two crewmen, Ted White and John Delaney, both close friends, didn't make it. "I'm afraid I was pretty much a sissy about it," Bush confessed in a letter to his parents, "I sat in my raft and sobbed for a while. It bothers me very much." Nearly half a century later, Bush would write, "It still haunts me today that I lived and two of my crewmen died."

Bush received the Distinguished Flying Cross for his actions that day. The citation reads in part, "For heroism and extraordinary achievement… Leading one section of a four-plane division in a strike against a radio station, Lieutenant Junior Grade Bush pressed home an attack in the face of intense antiaircraft fire. Although his plane was hit and set afire at the beginning of his dive, he continued his plunge toward the target and succeeded in scoring damaging bomb hits before bailing out…" The US military never captured Chichi Jima or its neighboring islands. When World War II ended, some 25,000 Japanese troops stationed there surrendered. **Facing page**, the September 2, 1944, deck log from Bush's aircraft carrier, the USS *San Jacinto*, reporting his rescue and the MIA status of his two crewmen. **Top left**, a contemporaneous photograph of the USS *Finback* on patrol. **Bottom left**, the crew of the USS *Finback* rescues Lieutenant Bush.

WEDDING BELLS: After a five-month secret engagement and a slightly delayed homecoming for Lieutenant Bush—Barbara had to scratch out the original wedding date on the printed invitations—George and Barbara were finally married on January 6, 1945, at the First Presbyterian Church in Rye, New York. "I haven't had the chance to make many shrewd moves in my young life," Bush wrote to his parents a few years later, "but when I married Bar I hit the jackpot." **Above,** Marvin and Pauline Pierce with their daughter Barbara. The bride wears mother-in-law Dottie Bush's wedding dress, circa 1921. **At right,** Barbara and the groom in his crisp naval officer's uniform.

▲ **POLITICO:** Prescott Bush, 51, in 1946. The following year, he would make his first serious foray into Republican politics, as finance chair of the Connecticut Republican Party.

◄ **TEMPLE OF FINANCE:** Partners of Brown Brothers, Harriman & Co., July 1, 1945: l–r, Thatcher Brown, Ray Morris, H. D. Pennington, Prescott Bush, Thomas McCance, and Knight Wooley. In December 1930, when *Time* magazine announced the merger of the dynamic Wall Street firm of W. A. Harriman & Co., founded in 1919, and the venerable Brown Bros. & Co., founded in 1825, it noted that eleven of the sixteen partners in the new enterprise were Yale grads. *Time* didn't mention that most, including Prescott Bush, were also members of Skull and Bones, the most prestigious of Yale's nine secret societies—as were *Time*'s co-founders, Henry Luce and Briton Hadden.
Photograph by Herbert Gehr

ON THE FENCE: Like many married war veterans, Poppy Bush hurried through college, finishing his economics degree at Yale in two and a half years. Still, he managed to serve as captain of the baseball team, following in his father's size-12 cleats. Under Bush's leadership, the Yale Bulldogs played in the first two (and Yale's last) College World Series, losing to the University of California in 1947 and to USC in 1948. Here Bush poses on a preserved section of the old Yale Fence (demolished in 1888), a prerogative reserved for team captains.

RUTH AND BAR: Top, on behalf of the Yale University Library, team captain George Bush accepts a gift of personal papers from baseball legend Babe Ruth. **Bottom**, young mother Barbara Bush watches her husband play ball in October 1946. Two months earlier, she had given birth to the couple's first child, future president George Walker Bush.

Skull and Bones, Secret Society, Yale Univ.

SKULL AND BONES: In the spring of 1947, like his father and two uncles before him, Poppy Bush was tapped for membership in Yale's oldest, most prestigious senior society, Skull and Bones. Selected by outgoing members for their athletic, academic, and social leadership, each incoming class of fifteen Bonesmen meets twice weekly in the complete secrecy of their forbidding brownstone "Tomb." All three US presidents who attended Yale as undergraduates—William Howard Taft, Bush 41, and Bush 43—were Bonesmen, as was the 2004 presidential runner-up, Senator John Kerry. Among the many unconfirmed and likely apocryphal rumors about the secret society is that clocks in the Tomb are set five minutes fast to remind members that they should stay slightly ahead of the rest of the world. **Top**, the Skull and Bones class of '48, with Poppy Bush just left of the clock. **Bottom**, the Tomb depicted on a postcard, circa 1912. **Right**, the 1948 *Yale Banner* yearbook, which summarizes Bush's distinguished college career.

WILLIAM FRANK BURTON, 3D (Billy), was born in Augusta, Ga., on July 27, 1927, the son of William Frank Burton, Jr., and Eva Katie Morgan Burton.

After completing his preparatory training at the Carlisle Military School in Bamberg, S. C., in 1943, Burton entered The Citadel. He went on active duty in the Navy in June, 1945, and was assigned to the training program at Yale from November of that year until March, 1946. He was a member of Trumbull College.

Burton was transferred to inactive duty in May, 1946, and discharged as an aviation cadet in June, 1947. He then returned to The Citadel, where he is taking the course in civil engineering. He is a member of the American Society of Civil Engineers and has taken part in intramural rowing. Burton, who expects to graduate from The Citadel in June, 1948, is planning to go into civil engineering. His permanent mailing address is Box 492, Aiken, S. C.

ROBERT DAVID BUSBY (Buzz) was born in Ada, Okla., on January 29, 1926, the son of Orel and Hope Threlkeld Busby.

He received his preparatory training at Culver Military Academy and in July, 1944, entered Oklahoma East Central College under the Navy Reserve officers training program. He was later assigned to Mississippi College and Duke University, where he became a member of Phi Delta Theta. Busby was released from the Navy in July, 1946, and in September entered Yale as a member of '48. He is now in the Class of 1947M. He has majored in government and is treasurer of the Student Council of Silliman College. In 1946 he won the intramural boxing championship.

Busby plans to study law at Oklahoma University and will later be associated with the firm of Busby, Harrell & Trice in Ada, Okla. His mailing address is Box 416, that place.

ALAN RICHARD BUSH (Dick) was born in Boston on January 14, 1928. He is the son of Herman Louis and Eda Gorfinkle Bush and is a cousin of Alan R. Finberg, '50.

In July, 1945, after receiving his preparation for college at the Boston Latin School, Bush enrolled at Yale with the Class of 1948. He is a member of Jonathan Edwards College and since 1946 has held the Gerald Robert Steinberg Scholarship. Since his Sophomore year he has been art director for the public relations department of WYBC, and in 1946 he directed the Intercollegiate Broadcasting System's radio survey at Yale.

Bush, who has majored in English, expects to receive his degree in January, 1949. Mail will reach him after graduation if addressed to 2009 Commonwealth Avenue, Brighton 35, Mass.

GEORGE HERBERT WALKER BUSH (Poppy) was born in Milton, Mass., June 12, 1924. He is the son of Prescott Sheldon Bush, '17, and Dorothy Walker Bush, a brother of Prescott S. Bush, Jr., ex-'44, and a nephew of James S. Bush, '22, George H. Walker, Jr., '27, John M. Walker, '31, and Louis Walker, '36.

In 1942, after graduating from Andover, Bush entered Naval Aviation. He later served as pilot in the Pacific and was awarded the D.F.C. He was discharged as a lieutenant (j.g.) in September, 1945, and entered Yale in November. Bush, who has majored in economics, was awarded the Francis Gordon Brown Prize in 1947. He was on the University baseball team for three years, being captain in Senior year, and on the University soccer team in 1945; he has both a minor and major "Y." He was secretary of the 1946 Budget drive and in 1947 served on the Undergraduate Athletic Association, the Undergraduate Board of Deacons, and the Interfraternity Council and was elected to the Triennial Committee. He belongs to Delta Kappa Epsilon, the Torch Honor Society, and Skull and Bones.

He was married in Rye, N. Y., January 6, 1945, to Barbara Pierce, Smith ex-'47, daughter of Marvin and Pauline Robinson Pierce. Their son, George Walker, was born in New Haven, July 6, 1946. Bush may be addressed at Grove Lane, Greenwich, Conn.

GO WEST, YOUNG MAN: "I am not sure I want to capitalize completely on the benefits I received at birth," Bush wrote in a pensive letter to a friend just before his June 1948 graduation. Instead, the young father, determined to make his own way, passed up a sure-fire Wall Street career and accepted an entry-level position at an Odessa, Texas, oil equipment firm owned by one of his dad's Yale classmates. After several moves, including a year in California, the family settled in Midland, Texas, a dusty town established by the Texas Pacific Railroad in 1881 as the midpoint between Fort Worth and El Paso. **Top**, the young family welcome visiting "Gampy" and "Ganny" Bush in October 1949. **Bottom**, at the Midland rodeo grounds in 1950 with "Georgie" and baby Robin.

IN THE SADDLE: "Georgie has grown to be a near-man," Bush reported in a letter to a friend in 1951, "talks dirty once in a while and occasionally swears. He lives in his cowboy clothes."

▲ **HATS IN THE RING:** In May 1953, newly elected senator Prescott Bush introduces the new vice president, Richard Nixon, to the sartorial pleasures of Panama hats. Eighteen years later, President Nixon would appoint Prescott's son, George H. W., as US ambassador to the United Nations, and in 1973 he would tap George to head the Republican National Committee.
Photograph by Michael Rougier

◀ **SINGING FOR VOTES:** After a successful Wall Street career and a three-year stint as finance chair of the Connecticut Republican Party, Prescott Bush, 55, first ran for the US Senate in 1950 as a fiscally conservative Republican. But in heavily Catholic Connecticut, his long-standing involvement with Planned Parenthood worked against him. (Connecticut prohibited the use of contraceptives until its law was ruled unconstitutional in 1965.) Bush lost to the Democratic candidate—fellow Yalie and Zeta Psi fraternity brother William Benton—by 1,000 votes. Two years later, Pres tried again, this time allying himself with World War II hero and fellow golf enthusiast Dwight Eisenhower. In a nationwide Republican sweep, both won. Here the candidate, a booming bass, and friends sing for votes on a local Connecticut television program during the unsuccessful 1950 campaign.
Photograph by Michael Rougier

ROBIN AND MOM: Pauline Robinson "Robin" Bush—named for Barbara's mother, who had died in a car accident two months earlier—was born in California in December 1949. At age three, Robin became listless and was diagnosed with leukemia, which was nearly incurable at the time. She passed away eight months later at Sloan-Kettering Cancer Center in New York after herculean efforts to save her life. She left behind her bereaved parents and two brothers: George, 7, and John Ellis "Jeb" Bush, 7 months. **Above**, two-and-a-half-year-old Robin with her mother—probably in her grandparents' yard in Greenwich, Connecticut.

ROBIN AND DAD: Eighteen months after Robin's death, George Bush wrote to his father-in-law, Marvin Pierce. "We still miss our Robin. At times Bar and I find ourselves vividly recalling the beauty and charm of our little girl. Time has not dulled these happy memories at all. I guess if we had Robin now we would just have too darn much happiness." **Left**, George Bush holds Robin in 1953, the year of her death from leukemia. **Above**, Robin's obituary in a Texas newspaper.

VIVA ZAPATA: In 1953, Bush joined his fledgling oil-drilling partnership, Bush-Overbey, with well-connected twins Hugh and Bill Liedtke to form Zapata Petroleum, named for the 1952 Marlon Brando movie *Viva Zapata!* The wildcatters struck oil with each of their first six land wells. Then, at Bush's instigation, Zapata became an early pioneer in offshore drilling. When Zapata split into two companies—the Liedtkes took the land wells, Bush the offshore operations—the twins merged Zapata Petroleum with several other oil companies to form Pennzoil. Zapata Offshore provided Bush, the ever-prudent husband and father, with enough personal wealth to enter politics in the early 1960s. **At left**, Bush boards an offshore rig in the Gulf of Mexico. **Above**, Bush and Hugh Liedtke in their Midland, Texas, office.

"THE LITTLE LADS": Bush's term, in a letter to his father, for, **l–r**, Jeb, 3; Georgie, 10; infant Marvin; and Neil, 1, in their Midland, Texas, home in 1956.

"A WONDERFUL FAMILY OF MEN AND BAR": Bush's description of his young family, in a letter written to his mother several years after his daughter, Robin, died in 1953. Here, Georgie, George, Neil, Barbara, Marvin, and Jeb Bush in Midland, Texas, 1957.

HOT HOUSTON SUMMERS: Marvin, Neil, Jeb, and Georgie Bush in 1959.

"WE NEED SOMEONE WHO'S AFRAID OF FROGS": Bush wrote to his mother after Robin's death, "We need someone to cry when I get mad, not argue.... We need a girl." His need was answered with the birth of Dorothy "Doro" Bush in 1959. **Front row**, Neil, Marvin, and Jeb. **Back row**, Doro in the arms of George W., Barbara, and George, Houston, circa 1962.

▲ **MASCOT:** This publicity photo of the Bush kids with a baby elephant (George W. was at Andover) was used in their father's first venture into electoral politics: George's 1963 race for chair of the Harris County Republican Party. At the time, reliably Democratic Texas was just beginning to go Republican. Houston voted for Richard Nixon over Democrat John F. Kennedy in the 1960 presidential race, and Republican John Tower took over Vice President Lyndon Johnson's Senate seat, becoming the first Republican senator from Texas since Reconstruction. Bush "decided to start small, very small," as Republican chair in Houston, but he saw the potential for a statewide Republican makeover earlier than most.

▶ **HIS FATHER'S FOOTSTEPS:** In the Bushes' Houston living room, 1964. While his father, Prescott, served three years as Connecticut Republican Party finance chair before making his first Senate bid, George took the plunge after only a year, challenging Democratic incumbent Ralph Yarborough. In the rough-and-tumble GOP primary, right-wing opponents painted Barbara Bush as "an heiress who spends all her time on Cape Cod." As Barbara remembered later, "I wrote my dad that to my knowledge I had never set foot on the Cape, and to please write immediately if I was an heiress." Like his father, George lost his first Senate race.

GEORGE WALKER BUSH
"Tweeds" "Lip"
5525 BRIAN DRIVE, HOUSTON, TEXAS

YALE
JULY 6, 1946

LOWER
AMERICA

JV Baseball 2,3; Varsity Baseball 4; JV Basketball 2,3; Varsity Basketball 4; JV Football 3,4; Head Cheerleader 4; Athletic Advisory Board 4; Student Congress 4; Spanish Club 2,3,4; Phillips Society 2,3,4; Stickball Commission 3,4; High Commissioner of Stickball 4; Proctor, America House.

Roommate: John Kidde

CHEERLEADERS

Bush, Booth, Sartore, Brown, Greene, Cowen, Townend, Franchot, Gonzalez.

ANDOVER: "Going to Andover was the hardest thing I did, until I ran for president almost forty years later," George W. Bush would later write about his boarding-school days. "I was behind the other students academically and had to study like mad." But Bush eventually made his mark at the elite all-male academy where, 25 years earlier, his dad had been an exceptional scholar-athlete. Although his grades were mediocre and his athletic performance undistinguished, Bush had a quick wit and well-developed people skills. His sunny disposition as head cheerleader and "High Commissioner of Stickball," **top**, would win him the runner-up spot in the "Big Man on Campus" contest.

GEORGE BUSH
CANDIDATE FOR THE
STATES SENATE

TEXAS POLITICS: In the 1964 GOP Senate primary, Bush tried to accommodate both mainstream Republicans and the right-wing John Birch Society by opposing President Johnson's civil rights legislation—widely unpopular in Texas—and the first US-Soviet test ban treaty, which easily passed the Senate. In a presidential election year when Democrat Johnson swamped Republican standard-bearer Barry Goldwater, Bush won the nomination but fell to Democratic incumbent Ralph Yarborough. Still, the 1.1 million votes Bush won represented the largest tally ever for a Texas Republican.

The dashing forty-year-old war hero won the Republican nomination with a lot of help from his wife. "She understood the intricacies of politics," brother-in-law Prescott Bush Jr. later recalled. "It was instinctive." Still, Barbara didn't always love the process. When George ran for Harris County Republican Party chairman, she took up needlepoint "to keep from looking and feeling bored to death. After all," she later wrote in her memoir, "I had heard George's speech two hundred times!"

D.C. OR BUST: The victory celebration at Bush's congressional campaign headquarters. In 1966, Bush sold his stake in Zapata Offshore to devote himself full time to politics. LBJ would later famously tell Bush, "The difference between being a member of the Senate and a member of the House is the difference between chicken salad and chicken sh*t." But for the time being, Bush lowered his sights to run against Dixiecrat District Attorney Frank Briscoe in booming Houston's newly created Seventh Congressional District. Bush won, garnering a solid 57 percent of the vote. So after eighteen years in Texas, the family pulled up stakes and moved to the nation's capital. "We had no idea," Bush later wrote, "that it would be twenty-six years before we would come back."

FOR COUNTRY AND FOR YALE: With oldest son George Jr. enjoying life at Yale—later, as president, he would jokingly tell graduating Yalies that even C students could aspire to his job—the rest of the Bush family navigated the tricky shoals of D.C. political life. "It was a whole different world for us," Barbara remembered, "exciting, overwhelming, intimidating, interesting, exhausting." The freshman congressman scored early and big when the Republican leadership, under Gerald Ford, appointed Bush to the powerful Ways and Means Committee.

MAKING THE ROUNDS: Bush calls on his future adversary, and later boss, Governor Ronald Reagan of California, **left**, and former president Dwight Eisenhower, **above**. Bush's father, Connecticut Senator Prescott Bush, was one of Ike's favorite golf buddies, despite the fact that the senator, who was the 1951 national senior golf champion and head of the US Golf Association, famously refused to let his president win.

PROUD FATHER: In the fall of 1968, while Congressman George Bush was cruising to a second term unopposed, George W. reported for flight school at Moody Air Force Base in Georgia, beginning his six-year, part-time career as a lieutenant in the Texas Air National Guard. Nearly four decades later, during the 2004 presidential election campaign, CBS newsman Dan Rather would report that the young flyer failed to fulfill his military obligations. Rather's evidence, however, was never authenticated. The newsman resigned, his producer was fired, and Bush was re-elected. **Above**, the former naval aviator and war hero pins lieutenant bars on his son. **Right**, the official portrait.

LOST CAUSE: In 1970, two-term congressman George Bush risked his safe seat in the House to take another crack at his Democratic nemesis, Senator Ralph Yarborough. He received overt encouragement from President Nixon, who promised to consider him for a high-level administration post if he lost, and veiled encouragement from former president Lyndon Johnson, who was no Yarborough fan. Bush correctly determined that liberal Yarborough had outstayed his welcome in increasingly conservative Texas, but he didn't grasp just how weak Yarborough was. Conservative Democrat Lloyd Bentsen—like Bush, a wealthy former World War II aviator and war hero—upset Yarborough in the Democratic primary, then beat Bush decisively in the general election. Bush would face Bentsen once more, in the 1988 presidential campaign, when Michael Dukakis chose the Texas senator as his running mate. **Above**, Bush with campaign interns during the 1970 Senate race. **Right**, Bush supporters in his hometown of Midland, Texas.

MR. AMBASSADOR: After holding out the possibility of a soft landing should Bush's 1970 Senate bid fail, President Nixon eventually delivered, offering the former congressman the cabinet-level post of US ambassador to the United Nations. Bush was not the administration's first choice. National Security Advisor Henry Kissinger initially opposed the appointment, and Bush got the job only after future UN ambassador and New York senator Daniel Patrick Moynihan turned it down **Above**, George Bush and his father, former senator Prescott Bush, in front of the US Mission to the United Nations in New York. The patriarch died of lung cancer soon after.

TWO CHINAS: During Ambassador Bush's first year in New York, the "two Chinas" issue was front and center. Bush spearheaded the effort to exclude Beijing from the United Nations and secure Taiwan's position as China's sole representative, only to be surprised by Nixon's sudden presidential visit to Beijing. "I think history will show the Nixon initiative to Peking is the thing that lost the UN," Bush wrote at the time. "I had my heart and soul wrapped up in the policy of keeping Taiwan from being ejected." **Top**, Bush confers with his boss, President Nixon, in the Oval Office. **Bottom**, he listens to a speech at the United Nations. Next to him is future UN ambassador and US senator from New York Daniel Patrick Moynihan.

A YEAR ABROAD: After President Nixon's resignation in 1974, Bush's many political friends worked hard to convince Nixon's replacement, Gerald Ford, to appoint Republican National Committee Chairman Bush as his vice president. When Ford instead tapped former New York governor Nelson Rockefeller, he offered Bush his choice of European ambassadorships as a consolation prize. Bush surprised the president by picking China, where he spent most of 1975 as chief of the new US Liaison Office. "We did not have diplomatic relations, which meant I would not be an ambassador but a 'liaison officer,'" Bush later wrote, "but I felt China was so important to our future, and a bigger diplomatic challenge than even Great Britain or France." Barbara wrote copiously about the jam-packed year, with its countless receptions, tours, and visits from dignitaries, family, and friends. "Everyone wanted to come to China," she noted. **Top**, Barbara writes down a recipe in the liaison office kitchen. **Bottom**, George W. and Doro visit Beijing during the summer of 1975. **Right**, George and Barbara, who adopted the local practice of traveling by bicycle, in front of the portrait of Chinese leader Mao Zedong in Tiananmen Square.

PATRIOTIC DUTY: In late 1975, President Ford recalled George Bush from China to take over the troubled Central Intelligence Agency, then under investigation in both houses of Congress for abuse of power. Although Ford rejected Bush as his vice president in 1974, he had noticed Bush's steady demeanor as RNC chairman during the turbulent Watergate scandal and his deft diplomatic skills in Beijing. Bush knew as well as anyone that the CIA appointment might end his political career—no CIA director had ever been subsequently elected to high office—but he considered it his patriotic duty to accept. "There is ugliness and turmoil swirling around the agency obscuring its fundamental importance to our country," Bush wrote at the time of his appointment. "I feel I must try to help." Widely credited with restoring agency morale, Bush held the demanding job until Democrat Jimmy Carter took office in January 1977. **Facing page**, Bush and Secretary of State Henry Kissinger confer in Beijing. **Top**, Supreme Court Justice Potter Stewart swears in fellow Yalie and Bonesman George Bush as director of central intelligence on January 10, 1976, while Barbara Bush and President Ford look on. **Bottom**, CIA Director Bush addresses agency employees.

George Bush for Congress

ON NOVEMBER 7,
VOTE FOR WEST TEXAS.
VOTE FOR
George Bush for Congress

Dear Voters,

Laura and I would like to take this opportunity to thank you for the many kindnesses you've shown us during my campaign for the Congress.

You've listened to me, and you've told me what you think. And hundreds of you have actively worked in my campaign.

I am very grateful to all of you.

During the past twelve months I have told you how much I want to represent you in the Congress. I mean that. I know I can do a good job.

Again, our thanks.

George W. Bush

THE FAMILY BUSINESS: On November 5, 1977, after a whirlwind three-month romance, George W. Bush, 31, married school librarian Laura Welch, also 31. The following year he ran for Congress, aiming to replace retiring Democrat George McMahon, who had served northwest Texas's Nineteenth Congressional District since 1935. George W. won the Republican primary but fell short in the general election when his Democratic opponent, Kent Hance, mercilessly attacked his East Coast connections and elite education. "I learned," Bush later wrote, "that allowing your opponent to define you is one of the biggest mistakes you can make in a campaign."

While George W. ran for Congress in west Texas, his father, back in Houston after a one-year stint at the CIA, decided to run for president. To some, it was a surprising decision. When son Jeb Bush, working in Venezuela for Texas Commerce Bank at the time, heard the news on the phone, he asked, "President of what?" The high point of the campaign came early, on January 21, 1980, when Bush upset front-runner Ronald Reagan in the Iowa caucuses. But in the long run, Bush's message proved too heavy on résumé and too light on political philosophy. He lost New Hampshire, won surprise victories in Michigan and Pennsylvania, and coined the term "voodoo economics" to describe Reagan's promise to cut taxes and expand the military simultaneously. Then he pulled out of the race just before the California primary, ceding the Republican nomination to the former governor and Hollywood actor.

RUNNING MATES: Newly sworn-in Vice President George Bush and President Ronald Reagan take the stage at a National Press Club gala in Washington, D.C., February 5, 1981. After more than a decade angling for the vice presidency, Bush won his place on the ticket when his longtime aide and campaign manager, James Baker III, persuaded him to quit the primary race early and graciously. The slot was nailed down when Bush agreed to support Reagan's campaign positions favoring tax cuts and banning abortions. Baker would become Reagan's White House chief of staff and treasury secretary and later Bush's chief of staff and secretary of state.

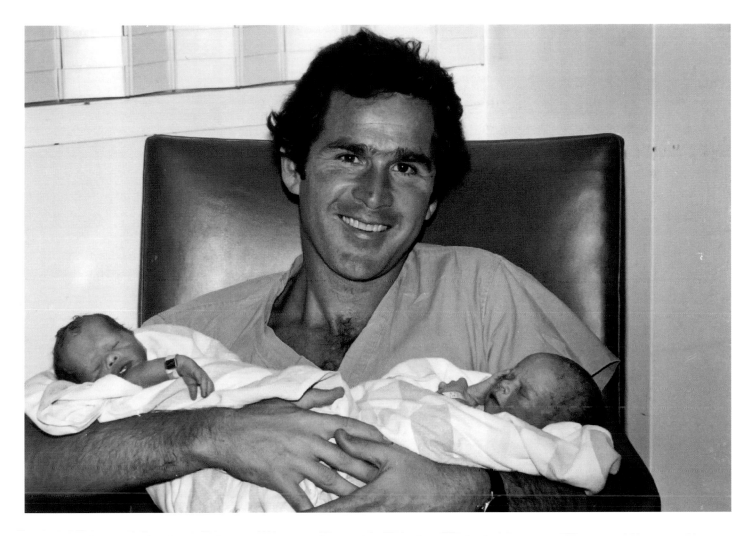

TWINS: "After a couple of years of trying, it was not happening as easily as we had hoped," George W. Bush later wrote, about the couple's attempt to have children. The Bushes decided to adopt, but several months into the process, Laura became pregnant with twins. **Above**, still at the hospital, the proud dad holds Barbara Pierce Bush and Jenna Welch Bush on November 25, 1981. The girls were named for their two grandmothers. "Holding Barbara and Jenna for the first time was a moment of incredible clarity," Bush wrote later. "I had been given a blessing and a responsibility. I vowed to be the best father I could possibly be."

THE VEEP: "President Reagan is a great man to work for and with," Vice President Bush wrote to a friend in mid-1981. "He gives me plenty of things to do, and he is a guy you can discuss things with without getting your head bitten off. We know the problems are immense, but I believe we can turn things around." **Top**, the vice president visits troops in Germany, 1983. **Bottom**, Reagan and Bush in the Oval Office and, **right**, strolling the West Wing Colonnade.

ALL PART OF THE JOB: Left, during the reelection campaign of 1984, Bush debates Democratic vice presidential challenger Geraldine Ferraro in Philadelphia. The debate, covering topics ranging from abortion to Central America, got prickly when Ferraro, the first female vice presidential candidate for a major party, called Bush's attitude "patronizing." In her memoir, Barbara Bush remembered the contest as being "very difficult. There seemed to be a double standard, one for [Ferraro] and one for George." **Top**, as president of the Senate, in 1985, Vice President George Bush swears in freshman Senator John Kerry of Massachusetts, while Kerry daughters Alexandra and Vanessa look on. Kerry would later challenge Bush's son in the 2004 presidential election. **Bottom**, the Bushes attend a British Embassy dinner in 1985 for Charles and Diana, the Prince and Princess of Wales.
Photographs by Terry Ashe (top) and Tim Graham (bottom)

FAMILY REUNION: The George H. W. Bush family at Walker's Point, near Kennebunkport, Maine, August 1986. Back row: Margaret Bush holding daughter Marshall, Marvin Bush, and Bill LeBlond. Front row: Neil Bush holding daughter Lauren, Sharon Bush, George W. Bush, daughter Barbara, Laura Bush, daughter Jenna, Barbara Bush, Vice President George H. W. Bush, Sam LeBlond, Doro Bush LeBlond, George P. Bush, Jeb Bush holding son Jebby, Columba Bush, and Noelle Bush.

▲ **CAMPAIGNER:** George W. Bush, 42, speaks on behalf of his father at a presidential campaign event in August 1988. A few months later, George W. would field a phone call that changed his life. The Texas Rangers baseball team was up for sale, and George W. wanted to be "the buyer of choice."
Photograph by Cynthia Johnson

▶ **KENNEBUNKPORT SUMMERS: Right, top,** in 1987, the morning flock of grandkids alights in the bedroom of "Gampy" and "Gammy" in Maine. **L-r,** Pierce, the vice president, Barbara, Jenna, grandma Barbara, Marshall, mom Margaret Bush, Jeb Jr., and Sam. Four years later, during Bush's presidency, a fierce fall storm generated thirty-foot waves that ripped a wall off this bedroom and washed its contents out to sea. **Right, bottom,** during the annual August family break—this one during George Bush's 1988 presidential campaign—Barbara and son Neil inspect a pot of steaming lobsters in the Kennebunkport kitchen.

ACCEPTANCE ADDRESS, REPUBLICAN NATIONAL CONVENTION

George H. W. Bush, August 18, 1988

I have many friends to thank tonight. I thank the voters who supported me. I thank the gallant men who entered the contest for the presidency this year and who have honored me with their support. And, for their kind and stirring words, I thank Governor Tom Kean of New Jersey, Senator Phil Gramm of Texas, President Gerald Ford, and my friend, President Ronald Reagan.

I accept your nomination for president. I mean to run hard, to fight hard, to stand on the issues—and I mean to win. There are a lot of great stories in politics about the underdog winning—and this is going to be one of them.

And we're going to win with the help of Senator Dan Quayle of Indiana, a young leader who has become a forceful voice in preparing America's workers for the labor force of the future. What a superb job he did here tonight. Born in the middle of the century, in the middle of America, and holding the promise of the future—I'm proud to have Dan Quayle at my side.

Many of you have asked, "When will this campaign really begin?" Well, I've come to this hall to tell you, and to tell America: tonight is the night.

◄ **SURPRISE PICK:** Presidential candidate George Bush with his youthful running mate, Indiana Senator Dan Quayle, at a New Orleans press conference in August 1988. Bush chose Quayle shortly before the convention without a family conference or an advisers' meeting. His longtime counselor James Baker, who considered Quayle insufficiently vetted, was not pleased. Quayle, the first baby boomer on a major party ticket and the son of a wealthy newspaper publisher, was quickly criticized for serving in the National Guard during the Vietnam War, thus avoiding the draft. "He kept his head high," Bush wrote later, "and was very loyal to me, and I never regretted my choice."
Photograph by Shepard Sherbell

For seven and a half years I have helped the president conduct the most difficult job on earth. Ronald Reagan asked for, and received, my candor. He never asked for, but he did receive, my loyalty. And those of you who saw the president's speech this week, and listened to the simple truth of his words, will understand my loyalty all these years.

Competence is the creed of the technocrat who makes sure the gears mesh but doesn't for a second understand the magic of the machine.

But now, you must see me for what I am: the Republican candidate for president of the United States. And now I turn to the American people to share my hopes and intentions, and why and where I wish to lead.

And so tonight is for big things. But I'll try to be fair to the other side. I'll try to hold my charisma in check. And I reject the temptation to engage in personal references. My approach this evening is, as Sergeant Joe Friday[1] used to say, "Just the facts, ma'am." And after all, the facts are on our side.

I seek the presidency for a single purpose, a purpose that has motivated millions of Americans across the years and the ocean voyages. I seek the presidency to build a better America. It's that simple and that big.

I'm a man who sees life in terms of missions—missions defined and missions completed. And when I was a torpedo bomber pilot they defined the mission for us. And before we took off we all understood that no matter what, you try to reach the target. And there have been other missions for me—Congress and China, the CIA.[2] But I am here tonight, and I am your candidate, because the most important work of my life is to complete the mission that we started in 1980. And how do we complete it? We build on it.

The stakes are high this year and the choice is crucial, for the differences between the two candidates are as deep and wide as they have ever been in our long history. Not only two very different men, but two very different ideas of the future will be voted on this election day.

---

[1] Sergeant Joe Friday was a character on the popular police drama *Dragnet*, which ran on both radio (1949–57) and television (1951–59 and 1967–70). Jack Webb, the creator of the series, played Sergeant Friday. Contrary to popular belief, Sergeant Friday never said, "Just the facts, ma'am." His actual catch-phrase was "All we want are the facts, ma'am."

[2] Bush had been a congressman (1967–71), chief of the US Liaison Office in Beijing (1974–75), and director of central intelligence (1976–77). He does not mention here his other significant positions: US ambassador to the United Nations (1971–73) and chairman of the Republican National Committee (1973–74). It was said at the time that Bush had "the best résumé in America."

And what it all comes down to is this: my opponent's view of the world sees a long slow decline for our country, an inevitable fall mandated by impersonal historical forces. But America is not in decline. America is a rising nation.

He sees America as another pleasant country on the UN roll call, somewhere between Albania and Zimbabwe. And I see America as the leader—a unique nation with a special role in the world. And this has been called the American Century, because in it we were the dominant force for good in the world. We saved Europe, cured polio, went to the moon, and lit the world with our culture. And now we are on the verge of a new century, and what country's name will it bear? I say it will be another American century.

Our work is not done. Our force is not spent. There are those who say there isn't much of a difference this year, but America, don't let 'em fool ya.

Two parties this year ask for your support. Both will speak of growth and peace. But only one has proved it can deliver. Two parties this year ask for your trust, but only one has earned it.

Eight years ago, I stood here with Ronald Reagan and we promised, together, to break with the past and return America to her greatness. Eight years later look at what the American people have produced: the highest level of economic growth in our entire history and the lowest level of world tensions in more than fifty years.

Some say this isn't an election about ideology. It's an election about competence. Well, it's nice of them to want to play on our field. But this election isn't only about competence, for competence is a narrow ideal. Competence makes the trains run on time but doesn't know where they're going. Competence is the creed of the technocrat who makes sure the gears mesh but doesn't for a second understand the magic of the machine. The truth is this election is about the beliefs we share, the values that we honor, and the principles we hold dear.

But since someone brought up competence, consider the size of our triumph: a record number of Americans at work, a record high percentage of our people with jobs, a record high rate of new businesses, a record high rate of real personal income. These are the facts. And one way you know our opponents know the facts is that to attack our record they have to misrepresent it. They call it a Swiss cheese economy. Well, that's the way it may look to the three blind mice. But when they were in charge, it was all holes and no cheese.

You know the litany: Inflation was 13 percent when we came in. We got it down to four. Interest rates were more than 21. We cut 'em in half. Unemployment was up and climbing,[3] and now it's the lowest in fourteen years.

My friends, eight years ago this economy was flat on its back, intensive care. And we came in and gave it emergency treatment, and got the temperature down by lowering regulation, and got the blood pressure down when we lowered taxes. And pretty soon the patient was

[3] Unemployment rose sharply, from 5.8 percent to 9.7 percent, during the first three years of the Reagan-Bush administration, and then dropped steadily to 5.5 percent by 1988, according to the Bureau of Labor Statistics.

up, back on his feet and stronger than ever. And now, who do we hear knocking on the door but the same doctors who made him sick. And they're telling us to put them in charge of the case again. My friends, they're lucky we don't hit 'em with a malpractice suit!

We've created 17 million new jobs the past five years—more than twice as many as Europe and Japan combined, and they're good jobs. The majority of them created in the past six years paid an average of more than $22,000 a year. And someone better take a message to Michael.[4] Tell him that we have been creating good jobs at good wages. The fact is, they talk and we deliver. They promise, and we perform.

And there are millions of young Americans in their twenties who barely remember the days of gas lines and unemployment lines. And now they're marrying and starting careers. And to those young people I say, "You have the opportunity you deserve, and I'm not going to let them take it away from you."

The leaders of this expansion have been the women of America, who helped create the new jobs and filled two out of every three of them. And to the women of America I say: You know better than anyone that equality begins with economic empowerment. You're gaining economic power, and I'm not going to let them take it away from you.

There are millions of Americans who were brutalized by inflation. We arrested it—and we're not going to let it out on furlough.[5, 6] And we're going to keep that Social Security trust fund sound, and out of reach of the big spenders. To America's elderly, I say once again: "You have the security that is your right, and I'm not going to let them take it away from you."

I know the liberal Democrats are worried about the economy. They're worried it's gonna remain strong. And they're right, it is. With the right leadership it will remain strong. But let's be frank. Things aren't perfect in this country. There are people who haven't tasted the fruits of the expansion. I've talked to farmers about the bills they can't pay, and I've been to the factories that feel the strain of change. And I've seen the urban children who play amidst the shattered glass and shattered lives. And there are the homeless. And you know, it doesn't do any good to debate endlessly which policy mistake of the '70s is responsive [sic]. They're there. And we have to help them.

But what we must remember if we are to be responsible—and compassionate—is that economic growth is the key to our endeavors. I want growth that stays, that broadens, that

[4] Bush's Democratic opponent in the 1988 presidential race was former Massachusetts governor Michael Dukakis. "Message to Michael" was a 1966 hit song by Dionne Warwick.

[5] Use of the word "furlough" here is intentional. In 1976, while governor of Massachusetts, Dukakis vetoed a bill that would have banned prison furloughs for first-degree murderers. A decade later, inmate Willie Horton, while serving a life sentence for first-degree murder, committed heinous crimes during a weekend furlough. Republican ad campaigns linked Dukakis to Horton, which helped Bush overcome a seventeen-point deficit in early public opinion polls. Bush's 1988 campaign manager, Lee Atwater, famously said of Dukakis, "I [will] make Willie Horton his running mate."

[6] The Reagan-Bush administration effectively cut inflation in half while adding 16 million jobs.

touches, finally, all Americans, from the hollows of Kentucky to the sunlit streets of Denver, from the suburbs of Chicago to the broad avenues of New York, and from the oil fields of Oklahoma to the farms of the Great Plains.

And can we do it? Of course we can. We know how. We've done it. And if we continue to grow at our current rate, we will be able to produce 30 million jobs in the next eight years.[7] And we will do it—by maintaining our commitment to free and fair trade, by keeping government spending down, and by keeping taxes down.

This is America: a brilliant diversity spread like stars, like a thousand points of light in a broad and peaceful sky.

Our economic life is not the only test of our success. One issue overwhelms all the others, and that's the issue of peace. And look at the world on this bright August night. The spirit of democracy is sweeping the Pacific Rim. China feels the winds of change. New democracies assert themselves in South America. And one by one the unfree places fall, not to the force of arms but to the force of an idea: freedom works.

We have a new relationship with the Soviet Union—the INF treaty,[8] the beginning of the Soviet withdrawal from Afghanistan, the beginning of the end of the Soviet proxy war in Angola, and, with it, the independence of Namibia. Iran and Iraq move toward peace.[9] It's a watershed. It is no accident. It happened when we acted on the ancient knowledge that strength and clarity lead to peace. Weakness and ambivalence lead to war. You see, weakness tempts aggressors; strength stops them. I will not allow this country to be made weak again—never!

The tremors in the Soviet world continue. The hard earth there has not yet settled. Perhaps what is happening will change our world forever, and perhaps not. A prudent skepticism is in order, and so is hope. But either way, we're in an unprecedented position to change the nature of our relationship. Not by preemptive concession, but by keeping our strength. Not by yielding up defense systems with nothing won in return, but by hard cool engagement in the tug and pull of diplomacy.

My life has been lived in the shadow of war—I almost lost my life in one. And I hate war; love peace. And we have peace. And I am not going to let anyone take it away from us.

[7] According to the Bureau of Labor Statistics, 2.6 million jobs were created during the four-year Bush administration.

[8] The Intermediate-range Nuclear Forces (INF) Treaty was a 1987 agreement between the United States and the Soviet Union to eliminate ground-launched missiles with ranges between 300 and 3,400 miles. By 1991, 2,692 such weapons had been destroyed—846 by the United States and 1,846 by the Soviet Union

[9] The Iran-Iraq War began when Iraq invaded Iran in September 1980, and it lasted until August 1988. The war caused an estimated 500,000 to 1 million military and civilian deaths.

Our economy is strong but not invulnerable, and the peace is broad but can be broken. And now we must decide. We will surely have change this year, but will it be change that moves us forward or change that risks retreat?

In 1940, when I was barely more than a boy, Franklin Roosevelt said we shouldn't change horses in midstream. My friends, these days the world moves even more quickly, and now, after two great terms, a switch will be made. But when you have to change horses in midstream, doesn't it make sense to switch to one who's going the same way?

An election that's about ideas and values is also about philosophy. And I have one. At the bright center is the individual. And radiating out from him or her is the family, the essential unit of closeness and of love. For it's the family that communicates to our children, to the twenty-first century, our culture, our religious faith, our traditions and history. From the individual to the family to the community, and then on out to the town, the church, and the school, and, still echoing out, to the county, the state, and the nation—each doing only what it does well and no more. And I believe that power must always be kept close to the individual, close to the hands that raise the family and run the home.

I am guided by certain traditions. One is that there is a God and He is good, and His love, while free, has a self-imposed cost. We must be good to one another. I believe in another tradition that is, by now, embedded in the national soul. It's that learning is good, in and of itself. You know, the mothers of the Jewish ghettos of the East would pour honey on a book so the children would know that learning is sweet. And the parents who settled hungry Kansas [sic] would take their children in from the fields when a teacher came. That is our history.

And there is another tradition. And that's the idea of community—a beautiful word with a big meaning, though liberal Democrats have an odd view of it. They see community as a limited cluster of interest groups, locked in odd conformity. And in this view, the country waits passive [sic] while Washington sets the rules.

But that's not what community means—not to me. For we're a nation of community, of thousands and tens of thousands of ethnic, religious, social, business, labor union, neighborhood, regional, and other organizations—all of them varied, voluntary, and unique.

This is America: the Knights of Columbus,[10] the Grange,[11] Hadassah,[12] the Disabled

---

[10] Named after Christopher Columbus, the Knights of Columbus is the world's largest Catholic fraternal service organization.

[11] The National Grange of the Order of Patrons of Husbandry, more commonly called the Grange, is a fraternal organization for American farmers. Founded in 1867 after the Civil War, it is the oldest surviving agricultural organization in America.

[12] Founded in 1912, Hadassah, the Women's Zionist Organization of America, is one of the world's largest Jewish organizations, with some 270,000 members.

American Veterans, the Order of Ahepa[13], the Business and Professional Women of America, the union hall, the Bible study group, LULAC[14], Holy Name[15]—a brilliant diversity spread like stars, like a thousand points of light in a broad and peaceful sky.

Does government have a place? Yes. Government is part of the nation of communities—not the whole, just a part. And I don't hate government. A government that remembers that the people are its master is a good and needed thing. And I respect old-fashioned common sense, and I have no great love for the imaginings of social planners. You see, I like what's been tested and found to be true. For instance:

Should public school teachers be required to lead our children in the pledge of allegiance? My opponent says no, and I say yes.

Should society be allowed to impose the death penalty on those who commit crimes of extraordinary cruelty and violence? My opponent says no, but I say yes.

I believe public service is honorable. And every time I hear that someone has breached the public trust it breaks my heart.

And should our children have the right to say a voluntary prayer, or even observe a moment of silence in the schools? My opponent says no, but I say yes.

And should free men and women have a right to own a gun to protect their home? My opponent says no, but I say yes.

And is it right to believe in the sanctity of life and protect the lives of innocent children? My opponent says no, but I say yes. You see, we must change. We've got to change from abortion to adoption. And let me tell you this: Barbara and I have an adopted granddaughter. And the day of her christening we wept with joy. I thank God that her parents chose life.

I'm the one who believes it is a scandal to give a weekend furlough to a hardened first-degree killer who hasn't even served enough time to be eligible for parole.[16]

I'm the one who says a drug dealer who is responsible for the death of a policeman should be subject to capital punishment.

---

[13] The American Hellenic Educational Progressive Association (AHEPA) is a service organization founded in 1922 in Atlanta, Georgia, to support Greek American charities and communities.

[14] The League of United Latin American Citizens (LULAC) was established in 1929 in Corpus Christi, Texas, to fight discrimination against Mexican Americans in the US Southwest.

[15] It is not clear to what organization Bush refers here, although it may be the Society of the Holy Name, a Roman Catholic lay fraternity associated with the Dominican Order.

[16] See footnote 5, page 78.

And I'm the one who will not raise taxes. My opponent now says he'll raise them as a last resort, or a third resort. But when a politician talks like that, you know that's one resort he'll be checking into. My opponent won't rule out raising taxes, but I will. And the Congress will push me to raise taxes, and I'll say no, and they'll push, and I'll say no, and they'll push again, and I'll say to them, "Read my lips. No new taxes."[17]

I want a kinder and gentler nation.

Let me tell you more about the mission on jobs. My mission is "thirty in eight"—thirty million jobs in the next eight years.[18]

Every one of our children deserves a first-rate school. The liberal Democrats want power in the hands of the federal government, and I want power in the hands of the parents. And I will encourage merit schools. I will give more kids a Head Start. And I'll make it easier to save for college.

I want a drug-free America, and this will not be easy to achieve. But I want to enlist the help of some people who are rarely included. Tonight, I challenge the young people of our country to shut down the drug dealers around the world. Unite with us. Work with us. "Zero tolerance" isn't just a policy; it's an attitude. Tell them what you think of people who underwrite the dealers who put poison in our society. And while you're doing that, my administration will be telling the dealers: "Whatever we have to do we'll do, but your day is over. You are history!"

I am going to do whatever it takes to make sure the disabled are included in the mainstream. For too long they've been left out, but they're not gonna be left out anymore.

And I am going to stop ocean dumping. Our beaches should not be garbage dumps, and our harbors should not be cesspools.[19] And I'm going to have the FBI trace the medical wastes, and we're going to punish the people who dump those infected needles into our oceans, lakes, and rivers. And we must clean the air. We must reduce the harm done by acid rain. And I'll put incentives back into the domestic energy industry, for I know from personal experience, there is no security for the United States in further dependence on foreign oil.

In foreign affairs, I'll continue our policy of peace through strength. I will move toward further cuts in the strategic and conventional arsenals of both the United States and the

---

[17] One of the best-known catchphrases in American political oratory, "Read my lips: No new taxes" eventually became Bush's single most troublesome campaign promise. When President Bush eventually agreed to raise taxes as part of a 1990 budget compromise with congressional Democrats, the reversal exasperated the conservative wing of the Republican Party. During the 1992 Republican primaries, conservative challenger Pat Buchanan employed the phrase extensively to challenge Bush, and in the general election, Democratic nominee Bill Clinton used it to impugn Bush's trustworthiness.

[18] See footnote 7, page 79.

[19] Another jab at Bush's opponent, Michael Dukakis, who as Massachusetts governor failed to clean up Boston Harbor—a body of water that Bush campaign ads accurately called "the dirtiest in America." Bush's boat tour across Boston Harbor two weeks after this speech was a public relations coup, and Bush pulled even in the polls in the governor's home state.

Soviet Union and the Eastern Bloc and NATO. I'll modernize and preserve our technological edge—and that includes strategic defense.[20]

And a priority: ban chemical and biological weapons from the face of the earth. That will be a priority with me. And I intend to speak for freedom, stand for freedom, be a patient friend to anyone, East or West, who will fight for freedom.

It seems to me the presidency provides an incomparable opportunity for gentle persuasion. And I hope to stand for a new harmony, a greater tolerance. We've come far, but I think we need a new harmony among the races in our country. And we're on a journey into a new century, and we've got to leave that tired old baggage of bigotry behind.

Some people who are enjoying our prosperity have forgotten what it's for. But they diminish our triumph when they act as if wealth is an end in itself. And there are those who have dropped their standards along the way, as if ethics were too heavy and slowed their rise to the top. There's graft in city hall and there's greed on Wall Street. There's influence peddling in Washington and the small corruptions of everyday ambition.

But you see, I believe public service is honorable. And every time I hear that someone has breached the public trust it breaks my heart. And I wonder sometimes if we have forgotten who we are. But we're the people who sundered a nation rather than allow a sin called slavery, and we're the people who rose from the ghettos and the deserts. And we weren't saints, but we lived by standards. We celebrated the individual, but we weren't self-centered. We were practical, but we didn't live only for material things. We believed in getting ahead, but blind ambition wasn't our way.

The fact is prosperity has a purpose. It's to allow us to pursue "the better angels,"[21] to give us time to think and grow. Prosperity with a purpose means taking your idealism and making it concrete by certain acts of goodness. It means helping a child from an unhappy home learn how to read—and I thank my wife, Barbara, for all her work in helping people to read and all her work for literacy in this country.

It means teaching troubled children through your presence that there's such a thing as reliable love. Some would say it's soft and insufficiently tough to care about these things. But where is it written that we must act as if we do not care, as if we are not moved? Well, I am moved. I want a kinder and gentler nation.[22]

[20] Probably refers to the Strategic Defense Initiative (SDI), Ronald Reagan's controversial "Star Wars" missile defense program. Though never built, the specter of SDI may have hastened the end of the Cold War.

[21] From the closing lines of Abraham Lincoln's first inaugural address: "The mystic chords of memory, stretching from every battlefield and patriot grave to every living heart and hearthstone all over this broad land, will yet swell the chorus of the Union, when again touched, as surely they will be, by the better angels of our nature."

[22] Another memorable phrase from speechwriter Peggy Noonan that burrowed its way into the national consciousness. Noonan had previously authored two of Ronald Reagan's most memorable addresses, those he delivered on the fortieth anniversary of D-Day in 1984 and after the *Challenger* space shuttle disaster in 1986.

Two men this year ask for your support, and you must know us. As for me, I have held high office and done the work of democracy day by day. Yes, my parents were prosperous and their children sure were lucky. But there were lessons we had to learn about life. John Kennedy discovered poverty when he campaigned in West Virginia. There were children who had no milk. And young Teddy Roosevelt met the new America when he roamed the immigrant streets of New York. And I learned a few things about life in a place called Texas.

And when I was working on this part of the speech, Barbara came in and asked what I was doing, and I looked up and I said, "I'm working hard," and she said, "Oh, dear, don't worry, relax, sit back, take off your shoes and put up your silver foot."[23]

Now, we moved to west Texas forty years ago, forty years ago this year. And the war was over, and we wanted to get out and make it on our own. And those were exciting days. We lived in a little shotgun house,[24] one room for the three of us. Worked in the oil business, then started my own.

In time we had six children. Moved from the shotgun to a duplex apartment to a house. And lived the dream: high school football on Friday night, Little League, neighborhood barbecue.[25]

People don't see their own experience as symbolic of an era, but of course we were. And so was everyone else who was taking a chance and pushing into unknown territory with kids and a dog and a car. But the big thing I learned is the satisfaction of creating jobs, which meant creating opportunity, which meant happy families who, in turn, could do more to help others and enhance their own lives. I learned that the good done by a single good job can be felt in ways you can't imagine.

It's been said that I am not the most compelling speaker. And there are actually those who claim that I don't always communicate in the clearest, most concise way. But I dare them to keep it up: Go ahead. Make my twenty-four-hour time period.[26]

[23] A month earlier, at the 1988 Democratic National Convention in Atlanta, Texas state treasurer Ann Richards had simultaneously ridiculed Bush's perceived lack of eloquence and his patrician lineage by saying, "Poor George. He can't help it. He was born with a silver foot in his mouth." Richards's line not only brought down the house but also brought her national attention. She was subsequently elected governor of Texas (1991-95), but was denied a second term by Bush's son, George W.

[24] A modest, narrow rectangular residence with doors at each end, the "shotgun house" or "shotgun shack" was popular in the southern United States from the end of the Civil War through the 1920s. The name may have derived from the notion that one could fire a shotgun through the front door and the pellets would fly cleanly through the house and out the back door.

[25] Bush's propensity to omit the pronoun I may be explained by this passage from George H. W. Bush by Timothy Naftali (Times Books, 2007): "His mother would remind him not to be self-centered, whenever possible not to use the pronoun I, and to avoid, at all costs, patrician pretension..."

[26] Bush pokes fun at his own ineloquence by purposely misquoting a famous line from the popular 1971 film Dirty Harry. As a criminal reaches for his gun, actor Clint Eastwood points a .357 Magnum pistol at him and snarls, "Go ahead. Make my day." Bush actually tripped over this line during his delivery, making the point clearer.

Now, I may not be the most eloquent, but I learned early on that eloquence won't draw oil from the ground. And I may sometimes be a little awkward, but there's nothing self-conscious in my love of country. And I am a quiet man, but I hear the quiet people others don't. The ones who raise the family, pay the taxes, meet the mortgage. And I hear them, and I am moved, and their concerns are mine.

A president must be many things. He must be a shrewd protector of America's interests, and he must be an idealist who leads those who move for a freer and more democratic planet. And he must see to it that government intrudes as little as possible in the lives of the people. And yet remember that it is right and proper that a nation's leader takes an interest in the nation's character. And he must be able to define and lead a mission.

For seven and a half years, I've worked with a great president. I have seen what crosses that big desk. I've seen the unexpected crisis that arrives in a cable in a young aide's hand. And I have seen problems that simmer on for decades and suddenly demand resolution. And I've seen modest decisions made with anguish, and crucial decisions made with dispatch. And so I know that what it all comes down to, this election, what it all comes down to, after all the shouting and the cheers, is the man at the desk.

I may not be the most eloquent, but I learned early on that eloquence won't draw oil from the ground.

And who should sit at the desk? My friends, I am that man.

I say it without boast or bravado. I've fought for my country, I've served, I've built, and I'll go from the hills to the hollows, from the cities to the suburbs to the loneliest town on the quietest street, to take our message of hope and growth for every American to every American. I will keep America moving forward, always forward—for a better America, for an endless enduring dream and a thousand points of light. This is my mission. And I will complete it.

Thank you. You know it is customary to end an address with a pledge or a saying that holds a special meaning. And I've chosen one that we all know by heart, one that we all learned in school. And I ask everyone in this great hall to stand and join me in this. We all know it.

"I pledge allegiance to the flag of the United States of America, and to the republic for which it stands, one nation, under God, indivisible, with liberty and justice for all."

Thank you, and God bless you.

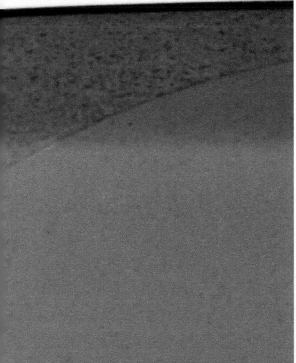

FRONT-RUNNER: In October 1987, when Vice President Bush announced his run for the presidency, *Newsweek* ran a cover story about the candidate headlined "Fighting the Wimp Factor." A few days later Bush noted in his diary, "The handlers want me to be tough now, pick a fight with somebody.... Maybe they're right, but this is a hell of a time in life to start being something I'm not." **Left**, campaigning in New Hampshire before the first-in-the-nation primary, Bush pledged not to raise taxes of any kind and beat rival Bob Dole by nine percentage points, cementing his front-runner status. **Top**, in Washington, D.C., the Reagans and Bushes join hands after the popular two-term president endorsed his vice president's campaign to succeed him. **Bottom**, in Miami, Bush sits down with mother Dottie Bush and conservative icon Barry Goldwater, whose endorsement had helped Bush win the New Hampshire primary a few weeks earlier.

▲ DEBATE DOMINANCE: At the second presidential debate, held in Los Angeles on October 13, 1988, Bush dominated opponent Michael Dukakis, the Democratic governor of Massachusetts. "Once I got out there," Bush noted in his diary later that night, "I relaxed, smiled and looked at the audience, and I felt much more comfortable than before." Bush scored points when he assailed the low-key technocrat as "a liberal, a traditional liberal, a progressive liberal Democrat" who, if elected, would unleash "an army of IRS agents into everybody's kitchen." Dukakis already looked soft on crime thanks to the Bush campaign's Willie Horton attack ads, which faulted the Massachusetts governor for a liberal prison furlough policy. Dukakis wounded himself further when he dispassionately opposed the death penalty even if, in the words of debate moderator Bernard Shaw, his wife, Kitty, "were raped and murdered." The Democratic candidate came off as a cold fish, his national poll numbers slipped, and the Bush-Quayle ticket went on to win the November 8 election with 53.4 percent of the vote.

▶ THE HOME STRETCH: A month before the election, the candidate rallies an enthusiastic crowd in Medina, Ohio.

A PAGE TURNS: "Some see leadership as high drama, and the sound of trumpets calling," the newly elected president said in his inaugural speech, "and sometimes it is that. But I see history as a book with many pages, and each day we fill a page with acts of hopefulness and meaning. The new breeze blows, a page turns, the story unfolds. And so today a chapter begins, a small and stately story of unity, diversity, and generosity—shared, and written, together." **Left**, the inauguration ceremony at the US Capitol. **Above**, US Supreme Court Chief Justice William Rehnquist administers the oath of office to the forty-first president while Barbara Bush holds two Bibles—one used by George Washington exactly two hundred years earlier and another open to the Beatitudes, Gospel of Luke version.

▲ **SMILE:** A Bush granddaughter snaps a Polaroid of Barbara and the president-elect at a gala held the night before the inauguration.

◄ **HAIL TO THE CHIEF:** The president and the First Lady make a dramatic entrance at one of the fourteen inaugural balls they attended on the evening of January 20. Barbara's blue velvet and satin gown is now on display at the Smithsonian, along with the outfit's stole, bag, pearls, and her $29 dyed heels. "Absolutely the most uncomfortable shoes I ever owned," Barbara later reported, "[and] the blue dye came off on my feet…. That night, every inch of my body ached, as did George's."

Family, faith, friends, do your best, try your hardest, rely on your innate good sense, kindness and understanding of the American people. That is where a President gets his strength, I'm sure of it.

—PRESIDENT BUSH'S DIARY,
JANUARY 16, 1989

DIGGING IN: "Then it was down to business," Bush wrote about his first days in the White House. The new president's business included a burgeoning federal deficit, a brewing financial crisis in the savings-and-loan industry, a sovereign debt crisis in South America, the slow-motion collapse of the Soviet empire, and continuing unrest in Central America, not to mention a Democratic House and Senate. "I feel comfortable in the job," Bush wrote in his diary the day after the inauguration, "[although] I'm not quite used to being called Mr. President." Here, a week after his inauguration, the president and first lady settle into the Oval Office with Millie, their four-year-old springer spaniel.

DEFENSE: Three months into his term, the president consults with his national security advisor and close friend, Air Force General Brent Scowcroft, and his new defense secretary, Dick Cheney, who had previously served as Gerald Ford's chief of staff and then as a five-term congressman from Wyoming. Cheney was Bush's second choice for Defense. His initial pick, former senator John Tower of Texas, narrowly failed to win Senate confirmation. "Although I am disappointed about the Senate's vote on John Tower," Bush wrote to *National Review* founder and conservative icon William F. Buckley, "I am thrilled about our new Secretary of Defense." Cheney's close connection with the Bush family would span the next two decades.

LIGHT MOMENT: The president, the First Lady, and friends celebrate the Bushes' first White House Easter. Although the Easter Egg Roll has been a White House tradition since 1878, the Bushes added their own touch—eggs signed by the president and first lady.

Millie is a caring, loving and experienced Mother. If one puppy goes too far away, she nudges him over; she rolls him over; and cleans him up.

—President Bush's Diary,
March 14, 1989

PUPPY PATROL: On March 17, 1990, First Dog Millie made round-the-world headlines when she delivered six puppies—five girls and a boy—in the First Lady's second-floor office. A month later, the president took a photo-op stroll with the proud mom and her brood. The Bushes kept the male and named him Ranger. One of the females, Spot "Spotty" Fetcher (named for Texas Rangers shortstop Scott Fletcher), went to the George W. Bush family in Texas. Spotty and her family would return to 1600 Pennsylvania Avenue eleven years later.

▲ **ADA:** On July 26, 1990, the president signs the Americans with Disabilities Act into law in the White House Rose Garden. The transformative law was, Bush later observed, "really the world's first comprehensive declaration of equality for people with disabilities." Joining him are, **l-r**, Equal Employment Opportunity Commission Chairman Evan Kemp and advocates Rev. Harold Wilke, Sandra Parrino, and Justin Dart Jr.

▶ **CLEAN AIR ACT:** Five months into office, President Bush proposed sweeping changes to the nation's Clean Air Act that addressed acid rain, regional air pollution, and toxic emissions. More than a year later, he signs the 1990 Clean Air Act amendments into law at a White House Rose Garden ceremony on November 15, 1990. William Reilly, administrator of the Environmental Protection Agency, and Secretary of Energy James Watkins look on.

TOP: Left-handed President Bush—five of seven US presidents since Nixon have been lefties—installed horseshoe pits at both the White House and Camp David, and thereafter the president's guests were expected to pitch in. Singer John Denver in mid-pitch, June 18, 1989.

BOTTOM: Japanese Prime Minister Toshiki Kaifu scores a ringer at the White House pit, September 1, 1989.

TOP: Australian Prime Minister Bob Hawke tosses a horseshoe at Camp David on June 25, 1989.

BOTTOM: The president shows British Prime Minister John Major how it's done, Camp David, June 7, 1992.

SOLIDARITY: Nobel Peace Prize winner Lech Walesa, founder of Poland's Solidarity trade union, met George Bush in Poland when Bush was vice president and Walesa was struggling against Poland's Soviet-backed Communist regime. When they sat down again on November 14, 1989—this time in the White House private residence—the future Polish president had peacefully dislodged the communists in parliamentary elections. Bush recognized the earthshaking nature of Walesa's achievement and awarded him the Presidential Medal of Freedom. The next day, Walesa addressed a joint session of Congress.

THE WALL FALLS: On November 21 in the Oval Office, West German Foreign Minister Hans-Dietrich Genscher presents President Bush with a fragment of the Berlin Wall, originally constructed in 1961. Eleven days earlier, when the wall was falling, the president wrote in his diary: "Moscow warns me ... about letting this talk of [German] reunification get out of hand. It causes them real problems, but what I've been saying is, this is a matter for self-determination, and a matter for the German people, and I don't think [Soviet Premier Gorbachev] could object to that." In fact, the president's pitch-perfect response to the wall's collapse—supporting liberalization without gloating—has been widely praised by historians. "The longer I'm in this job," the president wrote at the time, "the more I think prudence is a value and experience matters."

There's no way I will be able to sleep during an operation of this nature where the lives of American kids are at risk

—PRESIDENT BUSH'S DIARY,
DECEMBER 20, 1989

A MAN, A PLAN, A CANAL: On December 15, 1989, amid rising tensions and a US military buildup, Panamanian dictator Manuel Noriega declared war on the United States. In response, Bush launched Operation Just Cause, the American invasion of Panama and subsequent installation of democratically elected opposition leader Guillermo Endara. "It's a major gamble," Bush worried in his diary three days before the attack. "We do not want to be an occupying power in Panama. World opinion will be difficult." The December 20 invasion took just nine hours, during which twenty-four Americans and perhaps a thousand Panamanian soldiers and civilians lost their lives. Noriega, who took refuge in the Vatican mission, surrendered on Christmas Eve, after US soldiers blasted the mission with high-decibel heavy metal rock music round the clock. On the day of the invasion, President Bush listens to an update in his Oval Office study with National Security Advisor Brent Scowcroft, **center**, and Chief of Staff John Sununu.

▲ **GREETING MANDELA:** After twenty-seven years in prison, newly freed anti-apartheid activist Nelson Mandela embarked on a triumphant US tour. Here Mandela, who would become South Africa's president four years later, visits Bush on June 25, 1990.

◄ **SURPRISE WIN:** During an intense four-day summit meeting in Washington with Soviet President Mikhail Gorbachev, Bush observed in his diary, "It's funny how in dealing with the Soviets we think we know a lot, but we know so little." Bush had reason to be surprised. During the course of negotiations, in a dramatic turnabout, Gorbachev suddenly accepted Bush's suggestion that a reunified Germany should be free to join NATO. A delighted Bush offered the Soviet leader a trade deal in return. Here Gorbachev, with interpreter, confers with the president in the White House's Red Room, June 1, 1990.

I feel tension in the stomach and neck. I feel great pressure, but I also feel a certain calmness when we talk about these matters. I know I am doing the right thing.

—PRESIDENT BUSH'S DIARY, AUGUST 6, 1990

WAR COUNCIL: On August 2, 1990, Iraq invaded its tiny oil-rich neighbor, Kuwait. The same day, the UN Security Council passed Resolution 660, which condemned the invasion and demanded Iraq's immediate withdrawal. The Arab League followed suit. "It has been the most hectic 48 hours since I have been President," Bush wrote in his diary on August 5. "The enormity of Iraq is upon me now. I have been on the phone incessantly." A day later, Bush wrote, "Dick Cheney goes to see [Saudi Arabia's] King Fahd and calls back. Fahd accepts [our offer] and invites our troops to come.... [British Prime Minister] Margaret Thatcher was sitting in the office when Cheney called. I confided in her and asked her to tell no one." Here, on August 8, the president discusses the crisis with, **l-r**, General Scowcroft, Chief of Staff Sununu, Secretary of State Baker, and Defense Secretary Cheney, just back from Saudi Arabia.

THE REIGN IN MAINE: Even after Iraq's surprise invasion of Kuwait on August 2, 1990, forgoing the Bush family's annual Kennebunkport retreat was unthinkable. So the crisis came to the rocky Maine coast, which welcomed an unrelenting stream of diplomatic visitors. It was here that Bush built his coalition. **Above**, twenty minutes after Jordan's King Hussein leaves Walker's Point by helicopter on August 16, another helicopter delivers Prince Saud al-Faisal, Saudi Arabia's foreign minister, to confer with the president and his staff. Earlier that same morning, the president's beloved uncle, Johnny Walker, died in a nearby hospital, minutes before the president was able to reach his bedside. **Left**, the fate of the world waits a beat as the president chats with granddaughter Ellie LeBlond in the Walker's Point dining room during a morning meeting with National Security Advisor Brent Scowcroft.

VISITING THE TROOPS: In the wake of the Iraqi invasion of Kuwait and at the request of King Fahd of Saudi Arabia, President Bush announced Operation Desert Shield, an unprecedented US military deployment to Saudi Arabia and the Persian Gulf involving half a million troops, an Air Force fighter wing, and two carrier battle groups. The president spent Thanksgiving 1990 in the desert visiting the troops. "The kids were fantastic; it was an emotional day," Bush told his diary. "I wasn't sure I could get through the speeches.... The kids look so young yet they are gung-ho."

STORMIN' NORMAN: General Norman Schwarzkopf, head of coalition forces, with his commander in chief in the Arabian Desert on November 22, 1990, two months before the offensive phase of the Gulf War, Operation Desert Storm, liberated Kuwait. "I had a long briefing with Schwarzkopf," Bush wrote in his diary, "And I am convinced more than ever that we can knock Saddam Hussein out early. I'm worried that the American people might think this will be another Vietnam and it isn't and it won't be."

BURDEN OF POWER: On January 16, 1991, the day before the US Air Force began bombing Iraq, President Bush walks the White House grounds. That night, he couldn't sleep. "I think of what other Presidents went through," he wrote in his diary. "The agony of war. I think of our able pilots, their training, their gung-ho spirit. And also what it is they are being asked to do."

FACING THE NATION: On the eve of Operation Desert Storm, the president addresses the nation. "Our objectives are clear," he said in his brief speech. "Saddam Hussein's forces will leave Kuwait. The legitimate government of Kuwait will be restored to its rightful place, and Kuwait will once again be free."

TOP: On January 16, 1991, the day before the US would bomb Iraq, President Bush discusses the matter with Egyptian President Hosni Mubarak, as Vice President Dan Quayle looks on.

BOTTOM: On the same day, with National Security Advisor Brent Scowcroft in attendance, Bush phones other world leaders. "I have never felt a day like this in my life. I am very tired," Bush wrote in his diary. "My lower gut hurts.... People keep coming up to me and saying, 'God bless you.'"

TOP: After weeks of aerial bombardment, Iraqi dictator Saddam Hussein refused to withdraw from Kuwait. A ground war was now inevitable. On February 22, the day before the invasion, Bush meets with John Sununu, Dan Quayle, Dick Cheney, CIA Director Robert Gates, and Jim Baker. It would all be over in four days.

BOTTOM: On February 27, near the end of Operation Desert Storm, General Colin Powell speaks to General Schwarzkopf in the field, while President Bush compares notes with British Prime Minister John Major. White House Chief of Staff John Sununu, CIA Director Robert Gates, and Defense Secretary Dick Cheney listen in.

NEW WORLD ORDER: On February 28, 1991, the US-led coalition of thirty-four countries successfully ended Iraq's occupation of Kuwait. After massive US bombardment, Iraqi Scud missile strikes on Israel, Iraqi incursions into Saudi Arabia, nearly 400 coalition deaths, and more than 20,000 Iraqi casualties, President Bush declared a cease-fire. The Gulf War was over. "I was convinced," Bush later wrote, "as were all our Arab friends and allies, that Hussein would be overthrown when the war ended. That did not [happen]."

Above, the president addresses a joint session of Congress. "Tonight in Iraq, Saddam walks amidst ruin. His war machine is crushed. His ability to threaten mass destruction is itself destroyed," declared the president. "Now we can see a new world coming into view, a world in which there is the very real prospect of a new world order. In the words of Winston Churchill, a world order in which 'the principles of justice and fair play protect the weak against the strong.'"

Left, in Fort Sumter, South Carolina, on March 17, the president and former Navy pilot singles out two pilot heroes for special recognition, Captain Dale Cormier and Lieutenant "Neck" Johnson. In a letter to his nephew John Ellis the next day, Bush wrote, "There are plenty of problems to go 'round; but the critics can never take away this wonderful feeling of pride and patriotism that has swept the U.S. of A."

▲ **SUMMER VACATION:** Texas Rangers co-owner George W. Bush, wife Laura, and twin daughters Barbara and Jenna join the annual Bush family pilgrimage to Walker's Point in August 1991.

▶ **WALKER'S POINT:** The nine-bedroom main house at Walker's Point was built in 1903 by George W. Bush's great-grandfather, George Herbert Walker, atop a compact, rock-bound peninsula on the Maine coast near Kennebunkport. A larger-than-life character, "Bert" Walker was a wealthy banker and investor who made his first real fortune in St. Louis investing in railroads. Now called Walker's Point, the multi-house compound has served the extended Walker and Bush families as a summer retreat for over a century. To keep it in the family, Vice President Bush bought the peninsula in 1981 from his late uncle's estate, a move that "turned out to be one of the best decisions we ever made," Bush later noted.

▲ **EXCLUSIVE CLUB:** Four former presidents, l–r, Gerald R. Ford, Jimmy Carter, Ronald Reagan, and Richard M. Nixon, join the sitting chief executive at the dedication of the Ronald Reagan Presidential Library in Simi Valley, California, on November 4, 1991—the first time five US presidents gathered in the same place. Reagan framed this photo as a gift to President Bush.

▶ **CHRISTMAS DOG:** On December 16, 1991, five-year-old Millie enjoys the Christmas decorations in the White House Entrance Hall. Although Millie was able to maintain her girlish figure during her time at the executive mansion, her son Ranger took advantage of an obliging White House staff to cadge treats. On February 6, 1992, Bush had to issue a tongue-in-cheek "ALL POINTS BULLETIN FROM THE PRESIDENT" asking his staff to take the following formal pledge: "We agree not to feed Ranger. We will not give him biscuits. We will not give him food of any kind."

"WORST OF TIMES": That's how Bush later described the run-up to—and results of—the 1992 election. Election year kicked off with the incumbent president inadvertently vomiting on the Japanese prime minister in Tokyo. And it only got worse from there. The US economy was in recession, unemployment rose to 7.8 percent, and Bush's grand compromise with congressional Democrats to reduce the federal deficit, which forced him to renege on his famous "Read my lips. No new taxes" pledge, came back to haunt him. Conservative voters, goaded by the likes of young firebrand congressman Newt Gingrich and conservative columnist Patrick Buchanan, revolted. Then Ross Perot, a savvy, fast-talking populist-billionaire who had clashed with Bush over the Vietnam POW issue during the Reagan administration, announced his run for president as a third-party candidate—a threat Bush underestimated. In April, four days of violent riots burned through Los Angeles after the Rodney King verdict. By July, Bush's approval ratings stood at 29 percent, a level that had doomed Truman, Nixon, and Carter. Bush's reelection prospects dimmed.

Left, to shore up his reelection team, which suffered from the 1991 death of strategist Lee Atwater, the president asked his oldest son, George W.—here at the White House—to join his campaign as a consultant. **Above**, the president and Mrs. Bush escort the new Russian president, Boris Yeltsin, and his wife, Naina, down the White House staircase to a state dinner, June 16, 1992.

ILL WIND: On August 24, 1992, Hurricane Andrew slammed into South Florida with 150-mile-per-hour winds and gusts as high as 175 miles per hour. Just as the slow response to Hurricane Katrina would cast a shadow over his son's second term in 2005, perceived indifference to victims of Hurricane Andrew weakened the president's reelection prospects. **Above**, Andrew's aftermath, and a message to the president—BUSH SEND MONEY—on a Homestead, Florida street. **Left**, President Bush prays for the victims of Hurricane Andrew at the Camp David chapel in Maryland, August 30, 1992.
Photograph by Najlah Feanny (above)

▲ **TOO LITTLE, TOO LATE:** The president gives the double thumbs-up as he boards Marine One late in October. "It's now Thursday morning and we're in Detroit, I think," the president wrote in his diary five days before the November 3 election. "Yesterday was an exciting day. We got the report that two polls had closed—CNN and I believe an ABC poll—to 2 points. People were running back and forth in the plane. The rallies had a new zip and life to them." But the late campaign surge would not be enough.

◄ **UPS AND DOWNS:** "Several times during September I noted in my diary that both George and I feel very good on the road and discouraged when we get back to Washington," Barbara Bush wrote in her memoir. "The reception on the hustings was great, but bad press 'inside the Beltway' got us down." The president waves to supporters during a 130-mile whistle-stop tour of Ohio and Michigan in September 1992.

FIRST LADIES: Upstart Arkansas governor Bill Clinton, America's first baby-boom president, won the 1992 election with 43 percent of the popular vote, defeating the incumbent, who garnered 37.5 percent, and independent Ross Perot, who took 18.9 percent. Clinton carried thirty-two states and the District of Columbia, while Bush took eighteen. Two weeks after the election, Barbara Bush receives Hillary Clinton in the White House private residence. "She was very easy to be with," Barbara remembered. "We talked about the office, the mail volume, and [the Clintons' daughter] Chelsea.... It's a big lonely house for one little girl." Later that evening, ailing family matriarch Dottie Bush passed away at age ninety-one in Greenwich, Connecticut, after a visit from her son.

NEW TENANTS: The president, Barbara, and Millie greet the president-elect, Hillary and Chelsea Clinton at the White House before their drive together to the inauguration ceremony at the US Capitol on January 20, 1993. "Why did we lose?" Barbara asked in her memoir. She answered first for her husband: "George Bush says it was because he didn't communicate as well as his predecessor or successor, but I don't believe that. I think we lost because people really wanted a change.... People were worried about jobs and the economy. There was an impression that George was more interested in foreign affairs ... which was not true."

There's too much life ahead, too much to do and to enjoy...

—PRESIDENT BUSH WRITING TO
TREASURY SECRETARY NICHOLAS F. BRADY,
DECEMBER 30, 1992

LOOSE ENDS: The president works at his Camp David computer a week before Christmas 1992. He wrote to his brother John, "I am adjusting to the realities. We are building a little house [in Houston]. We are planning for the future. I am beginning to see the bright side of things, but I will always regret not finishing the course."

DOVE HUNTER: Two months before his election, future Texas governor George W. Bush, shotgun at the ready, looks to the sky on the first day of the 1994 dove-hunting season near tiny Hockley, Texas. When his hunting guide shouted, "Dove!" Bush fired and hit his target—not, regrettably, a dove, but a federally protected songbird. Candidate Bush immediately reported the incident to the proper authorities and paid a $130 fine. He skillfully defused the matter by joking to reporters, "Thank goodness it wasn't deer season. I might have shot a cow."
Photograph by Paul Howell

▲ TEXAS RANGER: The gubernatorial candidate and team co-owner signs autographs at the newly opened Rangers Ballpark in Arlington, Texas. After a spotty career in the Texas oil patch, Bush worked for his father's successful 1988 election campaign, then returned to his home state and bought a share in the Texas Rangers baseball team. He served as the Rangers' popular managing partner for five years, during which time the team enjoyed four winning seasons and landed a new publicly financed ballpark. Bush later wrote, "Owning a baseball team [was] a dream come true"—even more so when he sold his ownership interest in 1998, netting approximately $14 million on his initial $800,000 investment—a windfall large enough to support his political ambitions.

Photograph by David Woo

▶ UPSET: George Bush, **top**, backed by Texas senators Phil Gramm and Kay Bailey Hutchison, campaigns in the 1994 Texas gubernatorial race. Then, George and Laura, **bottom**, celebrate Bush's victory on election night. In what the *New York Times* called "a stunning upset"—even his mother predicted he would lose—Bush convincingly beat Democratic incumbent Ann Richards with more than 53 percent of the vote. Richards had famously denigrated Bush Sr. during her keynote speech at the 1988 Democratic National Convention, but six years later, Bush Jr. had the last word.

Photographs by Bob E. Daemmrich (top right) and Shelly Katz (bottom right)

▲ **THE LIBRARY AND THE LIBRARIAN:** At the November 1997 dedication ceremonies for the George Bush Presidential Library at Texas A&M University, the former president poses with his son, the governor, and his daughter-in-law Laura, who earned a master's degree in library science and worked as a school librarian before marriage. The sculpture in the background, *The Day the Wall Came Down* by New Mexico artist Veryl Goodnight, depicts five horses jumping through the rubble of the collapsed Berlin Wall. Although President Bush prudently avoided any semblance of public celebration when the wall fell in November 1989 (so as not to upset Soviet Premier Gorbachev's fragile liberalization policies), he was justifiably proud that the wall fell on his watch. The former president unveiled a second casting of the same sculpture in reunited Berlin on July 2, 1998.

▶ **SHOULDER-TO-SHOULDER:** George and Laura Bush aboard their campaign plane during the Texas governor's 1998 re-election campaign. Two days later, Bush would crush his Democratic opponent, Texas land commissioner and environmental activist Gary Mauro, winning a record 68 percent of the vote and 239 of 254 Texas counties.
Photograph by Steve Liss

Six years ago I was president of the United States of America. Tonight, maybe, the father of two governors. How great it is!

ANOTHER GOVERNOR BUSH: Like his father before him, Jeb Bush started his career as a Republican party chairman—in Jeb's case, Republican chairman of populous Dade County, Florida. Also like his father, Jeb lost his first election—a narrow 1994 defeat at the hands of never-beaten Democratic incumbent Lawton Chiles.

But in 1998, John Ellis Bush came roaring back, soundly defeating Florida's lieutenant governor, Buddy McKay. Bush would serve two terms as Florida governor—the first Republican ever reelected to the post. When Jeb was elected and George W. reelected in 1998, it marked only the second time in US history that brothers simultaneously served as governors. (Two Rockefeller brothers—Nelson and Winthrop—served as governors of New York and Arkansas from 1967 until 1971.) **Left**, Jeb Bush, Florida's popular future governor, at a 1998 campaign rally.
Photograph by Steve Liss

▲ **LOVIN' THE GUV:** After taking the oath of office for his second four-year term as Texas governor, Bush gets a big hug from seventeen-year-old daughter Jenna as Laura and Jenna's twin sister, Barbara, look on. With the state's largest tax cut, widely praised educational reform, and a landslide second-term victory under his belt, the governor of the nation's second most populous state was now poised for a presidential run.
Photograph by Paul S. Howell

▶ **GEORGE AND JESSE:** In the East Room of Bill Clinton's White House, at the 1999 National Governors Association meeting, Governor Bush chats with former World Wrestling Federation star and Minnesota's Governor Jesse Ventura. At this event, a dozen of the nation's Republican governors enthusiastically urged Bush to seek the presidency.
Photograph by Paul J. Richards

FIRST STEPS: In Austin, Texas, on March 7, 1999, Governor Bush, **left**, announces the formation of his presidential exploratory committee, the traditional first public step in a White House campaign. Among those present are, **above, l-r**, Representative Anne Northrup of Kentucky; Laura Bush; and Dr. Condoleezza Rice, then provost of Stanford University, later Bush's national security advisor and secretary of state. At this point, presidential exploratory committees had already been formed by five fellow Republicans: Senator John McCain of Arizona, former Tennessee governor Lamar Alexander, Representative John Kasich of Ohio, Senator Bob Smith of New Hampshire, and political commentator Pat Buchanan. The crowded roster of Republican hopefuls would soon be joined by Bush 41 cabinet member and future North Carolina senator Elizabeth Dole, magazine heir Steve Forbes, conservative activist Gary Bauer, radio talk show host Alan Keyes, Utah Senator Orrin Hatch, and, briefly, Bush 41's vice president, Dan Quayle. Although his teenage daughters predicted he would lose, saying, "Dad, you're not as cool as you think you are," Bush quickly opened up a financial advantage over the rest of the field, raising a then-record $36 million in primary campaign contributions in the first six months of 1999.

Photographs by Akhtar Hussein (left) and Susan Gaetz (above)

PRIMARY SCENES: Top, on June 12, 1999, in Cedar Rapids, Iowa, the candidate hugs Dr. Rosanne Freeburg, an Iowa grandma for Bush. Moments earlier, Bush surprised the press corps and delighted supporters by announcing, "I'm running for president of the United States. There's no turning back." The blaring music as Bush exited the stage—Stevie Wonder's "Signed, Sealed, Delivered (I'm Yours)"—reinforced the message. **Bottom**, on July 4, Bush campaigns in Merrimack, New Hampshire. **Right**, on August 13, he speaks to reporters at a "Front Porch Picnic" in Indianola, Iowa. The next day, Bush topped the unofficial but closely watched Ames, Iowa, straw poll, capturing 31 percent of the 23,685 votes cast. Magazine heir Steve Forbes finished second with 21 percent.

Photographs by Tim Sloan (top), Damon M. Kiesow (bottom), and Luke Frazza (right)

FAITH-BASED: Three days before the Iowa caucuses, where the first Republican delegates would be chosen, Bush speaks at the Teen Challenge of the Midlands, a faith-based addiction rehabilitation center in Colfax, Iowa. The candidate, who had renounced alcohol and renewed his Christian faith more than a decade earlier, prevailed in Iowa with 41 percent of the vote, garnering ten delegates to Steve Forbes' eight.
Photograph by Timothy A. Clary

BABES IN ARMS: A week after winning Iowa, Bush fell to Arizona Senator John McCain in New Hampshire. This made the South Carolina Republican primary, the first in the South, a must-win. Here Bush does what campaigning politicians do, cradling seven-month-old twins Reagan and Riley Ammons of Columbia, South Carolina. After an aggressive campaign—McCain thought too aggressive—Bush trounced his opponent, taking 53 percent of the South Carolina vote. After that, Bush practically ran the table, winning forty-three of the fifty Republican state primaries.

Photograph by Paul J. Richards

RUNNING MATE: On July 25, 2000, in Austin, Texas, Bush introduces his running mate, Dick Cheney, who had previously served as Gerald Ford's White House chief of staff and as Bush 41's defense secretary.
Photograph by Harry Hamburg

NEW RIDE: On August 1, 2000, George and Laura show off their newly painted campaign plane in Columbus, Ohio.
Photograph by Timothy A. Clary

ALL IN THE FAMILY: At the Republican National Convention in Philadelphia, Governor Jeb Bush commits Florida's delegates to his big brother. As George W. Bush accepts his party's nomination, his proud parents get a shout-out on the big screen.
Photographs by Roberto Schmidt (left) and Mark Wilson (right)

ON THE ROAD AGAIN: The Republican standard-bearer, fresh from the convention, greets supporters at the Joliet, Illinois, train station.
Photograph by Rick Wilking

RIVALS: In Boston, prior to the first of three presidential debates, Bush shakes hands with his Democratic opponent, Al Gore. According to a Gallup poll at the time, more registered voters thought Gore won the debate. But the numbers also told another story: prior to the first debate, Gore held an eight-point lead; just after, it was a dead heat. "[Communications director] Karen [Hughes] told me Gore had made a big mistake," Bush later wrote. "He had repeatedly sighed and grimaced while I was talking. That was news to me. I had been so focused on my performance I had not noticed." But viewers did, and by the end of the third debate, Bush was perceived as "the more likeable candidate" by 60 percent of the electorate.
Photograph by John Mottern

PARTNERS: Top, George and Laura hug after a campaign speech in Albuquerque, New Mexico, late in the general campaign. George later wrote of Laura, "She didn't try to argue me out of the race, nor did she attempt to steer me in. She listened patiently and offered her opinions. I think she always sensed I would run. As she put it, politics was the family business." **Bottom**, Bush and Cheney at a campaign rally at DuPage Community College in Glen Ellyn, Illinois.
Photographs by Paul J. Richards

TOO CLOSE TO CALL: On election night, the candidate, his father, and his younger brother, Governor Jeb Bush of Florida, gather at the Texas governor's mansion to watch the returns. Initially, the major television networks called Michigan, Pennsylvania, and Florida for Bush's opponent, Al Gore. Bush did the electoral math and realized he had lost the race. Then Bush's chief strategist, Karl Rove, called the mansion to tell Bush, defiantly, that the Florida numbers were flawed. Around midnight the networks revised their earlier prediction and called the state for Bush. Al Gore phoned to concede the race. But then, at 2:30 a.m., Gore campaign chairman (and later Obama chief of staff) William Daley called again, retracting the concession and setting the stage for a legal battle that would end five weeks later in the US Supreme Court.
Photograph by Rick Wilking

▲ **PASSION PLAY:** With the presidency hanging in the balance and a seemingly unending series of rulings, appeals, and recounts playing themselves out, passions ran high among Democrats and Republicans alike. Here, three weeks after election day, Bush-Cheney supporters protest in front of Vice President Al Gore's official residence in Washington.
Photograph by Manny Ceneta

▶ **HANGING CHAD:** The Florida presidential vote was so close that Gore demanded a recount by hand in four predominantly Democratic counties. The recount was stopped and resumed several times as Florida Secretary of State Katherine Harris, the Florida Supreme Court, and finally the US Supreme Court entered the fray. Here, Judge Robert Rosenberg of the Broward County Canvassing Board uses a magnifying glass to determine whether a punch-hole ballot had been partially punched (a "hanging chad") or merely dented with the stylus (a "dimpled chad" or "undervote").
Photograph by Robert King

RESOLUTION: On December 12, the US Supreme Court overruled the Florida Supreme Court, effectively stopping the Florida recount and calling the election for George W. Bush. Democrat Al Gore, who won the nationwide popular vote by half a million ballots, lost where it counted, by one vote in the nation's highest court and by five votes in the Electoral College. Gore conceded the race the next day "for the sake of the unity of our people and the strength of our democracy." A subsequent study by the *Miami Herald* and *USA Today* determined that if the Supreme Court had allowed the recount to proceed, Bush would have likely won by 1,655 votes instead of the 537-vote victory officially recorded. **Above**, Bush strategist Karl Rove mans the phone at the Bush-Cheney transition office in McLean, Virginia, the day before the ruling. **Right**, newly elected vice president Dick Cheney watches President Bush's long-delayed acceptance speech.
Photographs by David Hume Kennerly

MOVING DAY: At the governor's mansion in Austin, Texas, the president-elect supervises house movers, directing individual boxes toward the Crawford ranch and Washington. Twelve days later, the Bushes would move into Mom and Dad's old house at 1600 Pennsylvania Avenue.
Photograph by Stan Honda

FULL CIRCLE: On December 19, 2000, President Bill Clinton and President-elect George W. Bush walk toward the Oval Office to discuss the transition. Clinton denied Bush's father a second term in 1992, but eight years later, the nation's highest office was back in the family.
Photograph by Paul J. Richards

THE ONCE AND FUTURE PRESIDENT: The president-elect answers reporters' questions at the US Capitol after meeting with congressional leaders. Behind him is a copy of Gilbert Stuart's Lansdowne portrait, which depicts George Washington, 64, declining a third term as president.
Photograph by Luke Frazza

INAUGURATION DAY: George W. Bush takes the oath of office, administered by Supreme Court Chief Justice William Rehnquist, then delivers his inaugural address on a cold, rainy Washington day. Bush promised to reduce taxes, improve America's schools, overhaul Social Security and Medicare, and strengthen the US military. "America remains engaged in the world by history and by choice, shaping a balance of power that favors freedom," Bush said. "We will defend our allies and our interests. We will show purpose without arrogance. We will meet aggression and bad faith with resolve and strength."

Photographs by Don Emmert (left) and Tim Clary (above)

Then the door to the Rose Garden swung open. I looked up and saw Dad. "Mr. President," he said. "Mr. President," I replied.... Neither of us said much. We didn't need to. The moment was more moving than either of us could have expressed.

—George W. Bush in
Decision Points, 2010

41 AND 43: For the first time, the forty-third president of the United States sits behind the Resolute Desk, a gift from Britain's Queen Victoria to the nineteenth US president, Rutherford B. Hayes. Bush later wrote, "Sitting behind the historic desk was a reminder—that first day and every day—that the institution of the presidency is more important than the person who holds it." Here, the newly inaugurated president shares the historic moment with his father, the forty-first chief executive.
Photograph by Eric Draper

TOWN AND COUNTRY: Top, on February 4, 2001, President Bush arrives at the South Lawn of the White House after spending the weekend at Camp David. **Bottom**, on August 7, 2001, a pensive president drives his Ford pickup at his central Texas ranch. Two days later, Bush addressed the nation from Crawford, announcing federal funding for research on sixty existing stem cell lines extracted from human embryos. "This allows us to explore the promise and potential of stem cell research," said the president, "without crossing a fundamental moral line by providing taxpayer funding that would sanction or encourage further destruction of human embryos." Bush later wrote, "For weeks before the speech, I had felt a sense of anxiety … with the decision made, I felt a sense of calm." **Photographs by Eric Draper**

THE FAMILY THAT PLAYS TOGETHER: President George W. Bush, Former President Bush and Florida Governor Jeb Bush on the 18th green, Cape Arundel Golf Club, Kennebunkport, Maine, July 2001.
Photograph by John Mottern

My plan reduces the national debt, and fast. So fast, in fact, that economists worry that we're going to run out of debt to retire. That would be a good worry to have.

—PRESIDENT BUSH,
FEBRUARY 23, 2001

TAX CUT: On June 7, 2001, in the East Room of the White House, President Bush, flanked by members of Congress, signs into law the Economic Growth and Tax Relief Reconciliation Act of 2001, the biggest US tax cut since the early Reagan administration. This sweeping tax bill simplified retirement plans, provided rebates to 95 million taxpayers, and lowered marginal income tax rates across the board until January 1, 2011. The first of two Bush tax cuts, the act made good on candidate Bush's signature campaign promise, but despite the president's optimistic predictions, contributed to a nearly 90 percent rise in the national debt over the course of two Bush administrations.
Photograph by Stephen Jaffe

RELIEF FOR AMERICA

◀ **EVERYTHING CHANGES:** September 11, 2001, 9:07 a.m., Emma Booker Elementary School, Sarasota, Florida. White House Chief of Staff Andrew Card whispers to the president of the United States, "A second plane hit the second tower. America is under attack." Approximately fifteen minutes earlier, as Bush walked from his motorcade into the school, Senior White House Advisor Karl Rove told him that a plane had crashed into the World Trade Center. A few minutes later, National Security Advisor Condoleezza Rice called the president on a secure line to tell him that it was a commercial jetliner. "I was stunned," Bush later wrote. "[I thought] that plane must have had the worst pilot in the world." But it was not until Andrew Card whispered into the president's ear that Bush understood the gravity of the situation. "My first reaction was outrage," wrote Bush. "Someone had dared attack America. They were going to pay." He then looked up and saw White House Press Secretary Ari Fleischer holding up a handwritten sign that read "DON'T SAY ANYTHING YET." Bush, who would be criticized for his lack of immediate response, later wrote, "I had settled on a plan of action: When the lesson ended, I would leave the classroom calmly, gather the facts, and speak to the nation."
Photograph by Paul J. Richards

▲ **TAKING ACTION:** The president moves to a nearby classroom and watches footage of the second plane hitting the tower in slow motion. Horrified, he consults with advisors from a secure line at Emma Booker Elementary School. Then he addresses the nation (and a shocked group of parents and teachers expecting a talk on education) in the school library. A half hour later, Air Force One was wheels up.
Photograph by Eric Draper

◀ **THE FOG OF WAR:** On 9/11/2001, the president, White House Chief of Staff Andrew Card, Press Secretary Ari Fleischer, personal aide Blake Gottesman, Senior White House Advisor Karl Rove, and others peer out the window of Air Force One. During the motorcade from Emma Booker Elementary School to the Sarasota-Bradenton International Airport, Bush learned that a third hijacked plane had crashed into the Pentagon. He directed Air Force One to fly to Washington. The Secret Service agent in charge overruled him and stood his ground, even after Bush declared, "I'm the president, and we're going to Washington." Instead, the presidential plane, code-named Angel, climbed to 45,000 feet and flew to Barksdale Air Force Base in Louisiana, then to US Strategic Command at Offutt Air Force Base in Nebraska. On the plane, the president and his staff heard a raft of false rumors that included a bomb at the State Department, a fire on the National Mall, a hijacked Korean airliner, a high-speed object flying toward the Bush ranch in Texas, and a threat to Air Force One itself. Only reports of the fatal crash of a fourth hijacked plane in central Pennsylvania proved true.

Photograph by Eric Draper

▲ **WAR FOOTING:** A serviceman at Barksdale Air Force Base in Shreveport, Louisiana, guards Air Force One. Upon landing, President Bush was hustled off the plane. Then, from the commanding general's office, he reached Defense Secretary Donald Rumsfeld at the still-smoldering Pentagon and raised America's military readiness to DEFCON 3 (DEFCON 1 is the highest, DEFCON 5 the lowest) for the first time since the Arab-Israeli War of 1973.

Photograph by Paul J. Richards

THE AFTERMATH: Left, on September 14, 2001, President Bush flies from Washington to New York, where he takes a helicopter tour of Ground Zero, the southern Manhattan area devastated by the 9/11 terrorist attack that toppled both towers of the World Trade Center, killing 2,819 people. **Top**, Bush visits Ground Zero, where he takes part in an impromptu exchange with the rescue workers. As the workers chant "USA! USA!," Bush climbs a pile of rubble and uses a bullhorn to thank them for their efforts. When some of the workers yell that they can't hear Bush, he responds, "I can hear you! I can hear you! The rest of the world hears you, and the people who knocked these buildings down will hear all of us soon!" **Bottom**, two days earlier, Bush visited the Pentagon. Joined by Defense Secretary Donald Rumsfeld, Bush condemned the terrorist attack, which resulted in 184 deaths, and praised the rescue workers at the disaster site.
Photographs by Eric Draper (left and top)

IN GOD WE TRUST

▲ **TOUGH WORDS:** President Bush, backed by House Speaker Dennis Hastert and Senate Majority Leader Robert Byrd, addresses a joint session of Congress nine days after Osama bin Laden's al-Qaeda attacked the United States. In his speech, Bush delivers an ultimatum to Afghanistan's Taliban government: "Deliver to United States authorities all the leaders of al-Qaeda who hide in your land … [or] share in their fate."
Photograph by Win McNamee

◀ **CONSTANT REMINDER:** In the Oval Office, President Bush holds Port Authority Police badge number 1012. Bush later wrote that during his initial visit to Ground Zero, "[A woman named] Arlene [Howard] reached into her purse and held out her hand. It contained a metal object. 'This is my son's badge. His name is George Howard. Please remember him,' she said as she pressed the badge into my hand. I promised I would. I served 2,685 days after Arlene gave me that badge. I kept it with me every one of them."
Photograph by Eric Draper

ADDRESS TO A JOINT SESSION OF CONGRESS FOLLOWING THE 9/11 ATTACKS ON AMERICA

George W. Bush, September 20, 2001

In the normal course of events, presidents come to this chamber to report on the state of the union. Tonight, no such report is needed. It has already been delivered by the American people.

We have seen it in the courage of passengers who rushed terrorists to save others on the ground—passengers like an exceptional man named Todd Beamer.[1] And would you please help me to welcome his wife, Lisa Beamer, here tonight. We have seen the state of our union in the endurance of rescuers working past exhaustion. We've seen the unfurling of flags, the lighting of candles, the giving of blood, the saying of prayers—in English, Hebrew, and Arabic. We have seen the decency of a loving and giving people who have made the grief of strangers their own. My fellow citizens, for the last nine days, the entire world has seen for itself the state of our union, and it is strong.

Tonight we are a country awakened to danger and called to defend freedom. Our grief has turned to anger, and anger to resolution. Whether we bring our enemies to justice, or bring justice to our enemies, justice will be done. I thank the Congress for its leadership at such an important time. All of America was touched on the evening of the tragedy to see Republicans and Democrats joined together on the steps of this Capitol, singing "God Bless America." And you did more than sing; you acted, by delivering $40 billion to rebuild our communities and meet the needs of our military. Speaker Hastert,

[1] When United Airlines Flight 93 was hijacked on 9/11, passengers with cell phones learned that the World Trade Center had been attacked with hijacked airplanes. Todd Beamer used a seat-back phone to reach a GTE supervisor. He told her that some of the plane's passengers were planning to jump the hijackers and fly the plane into the ground. His last words, directed at his fellow passengers, were "Are you guys ready? Let's roll."

Minority Leader Gephardt, Majority Leader Daschle, and Senator Lott, I thank you for your friendship, for your leadership, and for your service to our country. And on behalf of the American people, I thank the world for its outpouring of support. America will never forget the sounds of our national anthem playing at Buckingham Palace, on the streets of Paris, and at Berlin's Brandenburg Gate.

We will not forget South Korean children gathering to pray outside our embassy in Seoul, or the prayers of sympathy offered at a mosque in Cairo. We will not forget moments of silence and days of mourning in Australia and Africa and Latin America. Nor will we forget the citizens of 80 other nations who died with our own: dozens of Pakistanis, more than 130 Israelis, more than 250 citizens of India, men and women from El Salvador, Iran, Mexico, and Japan, and hundreds of British citizens. America has no truer friend than Great Britain. Once again, we are joined together in a great cause—so honored the British prime minister has crossed an ocean to show his unity with America. Thank you for coming, friend.

> *The terrorists are traitors to their own faith, trying, in effect, to hijack Islam itself.*

On September the 11th, enemies of freedom committed an act of war against our country. Americans have known wars—but for the past 136 years,[2] they have been wars on foreign soil, except for one Sunday in 1941.[3] Americans have known the casualties of war—but not at the center of a great city on a peaceful morning. Americans have known surprise attacks—but never before on thousands of civilians. All of this was brought upon us in a single day—and night fell on a different world, a world where freedom itself is under attack. Americans have many questions tonight. Americans are asking: who attacked our country?

The evidence we have gathered all points to a collection of loosely affiliated terrorist organizations known as al-Qaeda. They are some of the murderers indicted for bombing American embassies in Tanzania and Kenya, and responsible for bombing the USS *Cole*. Al-Qaeda is to terror what the Mafia is to crime. But its goal is not making money; its goal is remaking the world and imposing its radical beliefs on people everywhere.

The terrorists practice a fringe form of Islamic extremism that has been rejected by Muslim scholars and the vast majority of Muslim clerics—a fringe movement that perverts the peaceful teachings of Islam. The terrorists' directive commands them to kill Christians and Jews, to kill all Americans, and make no distinctions among military and

---

[2] The Civil War ended 136 years earlier.

[3] A reference to Japan's attack on Pearl Harbor, in Hawaii, during World War II.

civilians, including women and children. This group and its leader—a person named Osama bin Laden—are linked to many other organizations in different countries, including the Egyptian Islamic Jihad[4] and the Islamic Movement of Uzbekistan.[5] There are thousands of these terrorists in more than sixty countries. They are recruited from their own nations and neighborhoods and brought to camps in places like Afghanistan, where they are trained in the tactics of terror. They are sent back to their homes or sent to hide in countries around the world to plot evil and destruction.

Every nation, in every region, now has a decision to make. Either you are with us, or you are with the terrorists.

The leadership of al-Qaeda has great influence in Afghanistan and supports the Taliban regime in controlling most of that country. In Afghanistan, we see al-Qaeda's vision for the world. Afghanistan's people have been brutalized; many are starving and many have fled. Women are not allowed to attend school. You can be jailed for owning a television. Religion can be practiced only as their leaders dictate. A man can be jailed in Afghanistan if his beard is not long enough.

The United States respects the people of Afghanistan. After all, we are currently its largest source of humanitarian aid. But we condemn the Taliban regime. It is not only repressing its own people, it is threatening people everywhere by sponsoring and sheltering and supplying terrorists. By aiding and abetting murder, the Taliban regime is committing murder.

And tonight, the United States of America makes the following demands on the Taliban: Deliver to United States authorities all the leaders of al-Qaeda who hide in your land. Release all foreign nationals, including American citizens, you have unjustly imprisoned. Protect foreign journalists, diplomats, and aid workers in your country. Close, immediately and permanently, every terrorist training camp in Afghanistan, and hand over every terrorist and every person in their support structure to appropriate authorities. Give the United States full access to terrorist training camps, so we can make sure they are no longer operating. These demands are not open to negotiation or discussion. The Taliban must act, and act immediately. They will hand over the terrorists, or they will share in their fate.

---

[4] Originally dedicated to replacing the secular Egyptian regime with a fundamentalist Muslim state, Ayman al-Zawahiri's Egyptian Islamic Jihad joined forces with al-Qaeda in June 2001.

[5] The Islamic Movement of Uzbekistan is dedicated to creating a fundamentalist state, under *sharia* law, in the former Soviet state of Uzbekistan.

I also want to speak tonight directly to Muslims throughout the world. We respect your faith. It's practiced freely by many millions of Americans, and by millions more in countries that America counts as friends. Its teachings are good and peaceful, and those who commit evil in the name of Allah blaspheme the name of Allah. The terrorists are traitors to their own faith, trying, in effect, to hijack Islam itself. The enemy of America is not our many Muslim friends. It is not our many Arab friends. Our enemy is a radical network of terrorists, and every government that supports them. Our war on terror begins with al-Qaeda, but it does not end there. It will not end until every terrorist group of global reach has been found, stopped, and defeated.

The civilized world is rallying to America's side. They understand that if this terror goes unpunished, their own cities, their own citizens may be next.

Americans are asking, why do they hate us? They hate what they see right here in this chamber—a democratically elected government. Their leaders are self-appointed. They hate our freedoms—our freedom of religion, our freedom of speech, our freedom to vote and assemble and disagree with each other. They want to overthrow existing governments in many Muslim countries, such as Egypt, Saudi Arabia, and Jordan. They want to drive Israel out of the Middle East. They want to drive Christians and Jews out of vast regions of Asia and Africa. These terrorists kill not merely to end lives, but to disrupt and end a way of life. With every atrocity, they hope that America grows fearful, retreating from the world and forsaking our friends. They stand against us because we stand in their way.

We are not deceived by their pretenses to piety. We have seen their kind before. They are the heirs of all the murderous ideologies of the twentieth century. By sacrificing human life to serve their radical visions, by abandoning every value except the will to power, they follow in the path of fascism, Nazism, and totalitarianism. And they will follow that path all the way, to where it ends: in history's unmarked grave of discarded lies. Americans are asking: how will we fight and win this war? We will direct every resource at our command—every means of diplomacy, every tool of intelligence, every instrument of law enforcement, every financial influence, and every necessary weapon of war—to the disruption and to the defeat of the global terror network.

Now, this war will not be like the war against Iraq a decade ago, with a decisive liberation of territory and a swift conclusion. It will not look like the air war above Kosovo two years ago, where no ground troops were used and not a single American was lost in combat. Our response involves far more than instant retaliation and isolated strikes. Americans should not expect one battle, but a lengthy campaign, unlike any other we have ever seen. It may include dramatic strikes, visible on TV, and covert operations, secret even in success. We will starve terrorists of funding, turn them one against another, drive them from place to place, until there is no refuge or no rest. And we will pursue nations that provide aid or safe haven to terrorism. Every nation, in every region, now has a decision to make. Either you are with us, or you are with the terrorists.

From this day forward, any nation that continues to harbor or support terrorism will be regarded by the United States as a hostile regime.

Our nation has been put on notice: we're not immune from attack. We will take defensive measures against terrorism to protect Americans. Today, dozens of federal departments and agencies, as well as state and local governments, have responsibilities affecting homeland security. These efforts must be coordinated at the highest level. So tonight I announce the creation of a cabinet-level position reporting directly to me—the Office of Homeland Security. And tonight I also announce a distinguished American to lead this effort, to strengthen American security: a military veteran, an effective governor, a true patriot, a trusted friend—Pennsylvania's Tom Ridge.[6] He will lead, oversee, and coordinate a comprehensive national strategy to safeguard our country against terrorism and respond to any attacks that may come.

These measures are essential. But the only way to defeat terrorism as a threat to our way of life is to stop it, eliminate it, and destroy it where it grows. Many will be involved in this effort—from FBI agents to intelligence operatives to the reservists we have called to active duty. All deserve our thanks, and all have our prayers. And tonight, a few miles from the damaged Pentagon, I have a message for our military: be ready. I've called the armed forces to alert, and there is a reason. The hour is coming when America will act, and you will make us proud. This is not, however, just America's fight. And what is at stake is not just America's freedom. This is the world's fight. This is civilization's fight. This is the fight of all who believe in progress and pluralism, tolerance and freedom.

We ask every nation to join us. We will ask, and we will need, the help of police forces, intelligence services, and banking systems around the world. The United States is grateful that many nations and many international organizations have already responded with sympathy and with support—nations from Latin America, to Asia, to Africa, to Europe, to the Islamic world. Perhaps the NATO charter reflects best the attitude of the world: an attack on one is an attack on all. The civilized world is rallying to America's side. They understand that if this terror goes unpunished, their own cities, their own citizens may be next. Terror, unanswered, cannot only bring down buildings; it can threaten the stability of legitimate governments. And you know what? We're not going to allow it.

[6] Ridge was a Republican congressman from northwest Pennsylvania (1983-95) and then a popular governor of the state until Bush appointed him secretary of homeland security, a role he filled until 2005.

Americans are asking: what is expected of us? I ask you to live your lives, and hug your children. I know many citizens have fears tonight, and I ask you to be calm and resolute, even in the face of a continuing threat. I ask you to uphold the values of America, and remember why so many have come here. We are in a fight for our principles, and our first responsibility is to live by them. No one should be singled out for unfair treatment or unkind words because of their ethnic background or religious faith. I ask you to continue to support the victims of this tragedy with your contributions. Those who want to give can go to a central source of information, libertyunites.org, to find the names of groups providing direct help in New York, Pennsylvania, and Virginia.

Freedom and fear are at war. The advance of human freedom—the great achievement of our time, and the great hope of every time—now depends on us.

The thousands of FBI agents who are now at work in this investigation may need your cooperation, and I ask you to give it. I ask for your patience with the delays and inconveniences that may accompany tighter security, and for your patience in what will be a long struggle. I ask your continued participation and confidence in the American economy. Terrorists attacked a symbol of American prosperity. They did not touch its source. America is successful because of the hard work and creativity and enterprise of our people. These were the true strengths of our economy before September 11th, and they are our strengths today. And, finally, please continue praying for the victims of terror and their families, for those in uniform, and for our great country. Prayer has comforted us in sorrow, and will help strengthen us for the journey ahead.

Tonight I thank my fellow Americans for what you have already done and for what you will do. And ladies and gentlemen of the Congress, I thank you, their representatives, for what you have already done and for what we will do together. Tonight, we face new and sudden national challenges. We will come together to improve air safety, to dramatically expand the number of air marshals on domestic flights, and take new measures to prevent hijacking. We will come together to promote stability and keep our airlines flying, with direct assistance during this emergency. We will come together to give law enforcement the additional tools it needs to track down terror here at home. We will come together to strengthen our intelligence capabilities to know the plans of terrorists before they act, and to find them before they strike.

We will come together to take active steps that strengthen America's economy and put our people back to work. Tonight we welcome two leaders who embody the extraordinary spirit of all New Yorkers: Governor George Pataki and Mayor Rudolph Giuliani. As a symbol of America's resolve, my administration will work with Congress, and these two leaders, to show the world that we will rebuild New York City.

After all that has just passed—all the lives taken, and all the possibilities and hopes that died with them—it is natural to wonder if America's future is one of fear. Some speak of an age of terror. I know there are struggles ahead, and dangers to face. But this country will define our times, not be defined by them. As long as the United States of America is determined and strong, this will not be an age of terror; this will be an age of liberty, here and across the world.

We will rally the world to this cause by our efforts, by our courage. We will not tire, we will not falter, and we will not fail.

Great harm has been done to us. We have suffered great loss. And in our grief and anger we have found our mission and our moment. Freedom and fear are at war. The advance of human freedom—the great achievement of our time, and the great hope of every time—now depends on us. Our nation, this generation, will lift a dark threat of violence from our people and our future. We will rally the world to this cause by our efforts, by our courage. We will not tire, we will not falter, and we will not fail.

It is my hope that in the months and years ahead, life will return almost to normal. We'll go back to our lives and routines, and that is good. Even grief recedes with time and grace. But our resolve must not pass. Each of us will remember what happened that day, and to whom it happened. We'll remember the moment the news came—where we were and what we were doing. Some will remember an image of a fire, or a story of rescue. Some will carry memories of a face and a voice gone forever.

And I will carry this: it is the police shield of a man named George Howard, who died at the World Trade Center trying to save others. It was given to me by his mom, Arlene, as a proud memorial to her son. It is my reminder of lives that ended, and a task that does not end. I will not forget this wound to our country or those who inflicted it. I will not yield; I will not rest; I will not relent in waging this struggle for freedom and security for the American people. The course of this conflict is not known, yet its outcome is certain. Freedom and fear, justice and cruelty, have always been at war, and we know that God is not neutral between them.

Fellow citizens, we'll meet violence with patient justice—assured of the rightness of our cause, and confident of the victories to come. In all that lies before us, may God grant us wisdom, and may He watch over the United States of America.

▲ **BIPARTISAN EFFORT:** At Hamilton High School in Hamilton, Ohio, nine-year-old Tez Taylor asks President Bush a question during a bill-signing ceremony for the No Child Left Behind Act. The educational reform bill, mandating standards and accountability nationwide, became more controversial over time, but in 2001 it passed both houses of Congress with overwhelming bipartisan majorities. Behind the president are, l–r, Democratic Representative George Miller of Ohio, Democratic Senator Ted Kennedy of Massachusetts, Secretary of Education Rodney Paige, Republican Senator Judd Gregg of New Hampshire, and Republican Representative John Boehner of Ohio, who would become Speaker of the House in 2011.

Photograph by Tim Sloan

▲ **AIDS INITIATIVE:** President Bush acknowledges applause from cabinet members and congressional leaders during an East Room event publicizing his global HIV/AIDS initiative. First announced in his January 2003 State of the Union address, Bush's five-year, $15 billion initiative, known as the President's Emergency Plan for AIDS Reduction, or PEPFAR, was by far the nation's largest commitment to battling the global AIDS scourge. It was also, Bush would later write, one of his proudest achievements.

Photograph by Alex Wong

QUIET MOMENT: President Bush enjoys a contemplative moment outside the Oval Office on February 15, 2002. Earlier in the day the president presented, as an alternative to the internationally endorsed Kyoto Protocol on global warming, a voluntary plan to slow the growth of greenhouse gases. That day he also backed the Energy Department's recommendation to store 77,000 metric tons of high-level nuclear waste in an underground facility in Yucca Mountain, Nevada.
Photograph by Eric Draper

REDECORATING: George and Laura Bush tidy up the recently redecorated Oval Office. "There were new drapes and new beige and damask sofas, three in total, in case someone spilled coffee on one and the staff had to replace it in a hurry," Laura Bush later wrote, "There was a new pale wool rug with a sunburst pattern featuring the presidential seal, because George had wanted the room to say, 'An optimistic man works here.'"
Photograph by Eric Draper

◀ **CASE FOR WAR:** A year and a day after the 9/11 attacks, President Bush stands before the UN General Assembly and delivers a lengthy indictment of Iraqi dictator Saddam Hussein—in effect, his *casus belli*, or case for war, against the Iraqi regime. Among the charges: refusal to comply with numerous UN resolutions regarding persecution of his own people and return of foreign prisoners; abuse of the UN oil-for-food program; supporting al-Qaeda and Palestinian terrorists; attempted assassination of both the emir of Kuwait and Bush's own father—and most importantly, Saddam's refusal to cooperate with UN inspectors searching for weapons of mass destruction. "My nation will work with the UN Security Council to meet our common challenge...." said Bush. "But the purposes of the United States should not be doubted. The Security Council resolutions will be enforced—the just demands of peace and security will be met—or action will be unavoidable."
Photograph by Spencer Platt

▲ **BEFORE THE STORM:** On March 19, 2003, the day before America and its allies invade Iraq, President Bush and Spotty walk the White House grounds. His father took a similar walk the day before he launched Operation Desert Storm against Iraq, twelve years earlier (pictured on page 116). "Our last-ditch hope was that Saddam would agree to go into exile," Bush wrote, describing an offer from "a Middle Eastern government"—summarily declined by Saddam—to send the Iraqi leader, along with a billion dollars in cash, to the former Soviet republic of Belarus. "[But] the dictator of Iraq had made his decision," wrote Bush. "He chose war."
Photograph by Eric Draper

▲ **TIDINGS OF WAR:** On March 20, 2003, the 8:00 p.m. deadline for Saddam Hussein to leave Iraq passes. At 10:15 p.m. Bush addresses the nation from the Oval Office. "My fellow citizens," he said, "at this hour, American and coalition forces are in the early stages of military operations to disarm Iraq, to free its people and to defend the world from grave danger.... I assure you this will not be a campaign of half measures, and we will accept no outcome but victory."
Photograph by Alex Wong

▶ **WAR COUNCIL:** In the Oval Office on March 20, 2003, President Bush receives an update on military action in Iraq from, **l-r**, Vice President Dick Cheney, CIA Director George Tenet, and White House Chief of Staff Andrew Card. Baghdad would fall in three weeks.
Photograph by Eric Draper

BAD OPTICS: On May 1, 2003, in San Diego, California, President Bush climbed into the seat of a military jet for the first time in thirty years. After takeoff, Bush briefly piloted the Lockheed S-3B Viking, and then Commander John "Skip" Lussier landed it on the nuclear aircraft carrier the USS *Abraham Lincoln*. The president addressed the ship's crew—and the nation—from the carrier deck. "Major combat operations in Iraq have ended," declared the president. "In the battle of Iraq, the United States and our allies have prevailed." The premature nature of Bush's declaration—Iraq would take the rest of his presidency to stabilize, and no weapons of mass destruction would ever be found—was exacerbated by the made-for-TV banner hanging behind the president. "'Mission Accomplished' became a shorthand criticism for all that subsequently went wrong in Iraq," Bush later wrote. "My speech made clear that our work was far from done. But all the explaining in the world could not reverse the perception. Our stagecraft had gone awry. It was a big mistake."
Photographs by Brooks Kraft (above) and Stephen Jaffe (right)

BAGHDAD THANKSGIVING: On November 27, 2003, President Bush serves a Thanksgiving turkey with all the trimmings to US troops stationed at Baghdad International Airport. The war zone visit, which Bush and National Security Advisor Condoleezza Rice undertook despite considerable risk, was a closely held secret. The president and Dr. Rice left from Bush's Crawford ranch in an unmarked Suburban, baseball caps pulled low over their faces. Even some Crawford Secret Service agents didn't know they had left. Unable to risk a motorcade to the airport, the president of the United States was caught in his first traffic jam since assuming office.The takeoff from Baghdad—lights out, radio silence—was particularly dangerous but deemed worthwhile by a commander-in-chief who, throughout his presidency, enjoyed a special rapport with the troops.

Photograph by Tim Sloan

ABU GHRAIB: President Bush visits Secretary of Defense Donald Rumsfeld's office at the Pentagon to view photos of prisoner abuse by US soldiers at Baghdad's Abu Ghraib prison. Rumsfeld would twice offer to resign over the scandal, which Bush described as "a low point of my presidency." The president later wrote that he "didn't have an obvious replacement" for Rumsfeld, although Bush did reach out to Federal Express founder and fellow Skull and Bones member Fred Smith, who declined for personal reasons. In 2006, when Rumsfeld again asked to resign, Bush reached back to his father's administration to tap former CIA director Robert Gates. Vice President Dick Cheney initially opposed the choice, but its wisdom was soon apparent—even to Bush's Democratic successor, Barack Obama, who kept Gates on after winning the 2008 presidential election.
Photograph by David Hume Kennerly

TAX CUT 2: President Bush signs the Working Families Tax Relief Act of 2004 in Des Moines as Iowa senator Chuck Grassley and friends watch.
Photograph by Mario Tama

CONVENTION 2: President Bush shakes hands with his father, the former president, after accepting the Republican nomination for a second term at Madison Square Garden.
Photograph by Michael Appleton

DEBATE 3: In Tempe, Arizona, October 13, 2004, President Bush and opponent, John Kerry, acknowledge the Arizona State audience before the third presidential debate.
Photograph by Mario Tama

TERM 2: On election night, 2004, President Bush and the first lady are joined in the White House residence by daughters Barbara and Jenna, nephew Sam LeBlond, the former president and first lady, and the president's sister, Dora. Bush would take every state he won in 2000 plus New Mexico and New Hampshire—and this time, he would carry Florida decisively.
Photograph by Stephen Jaffe

KATRINA: On August 29, 2005, Hurricane Katrina slammed the Mississippi and Louisiana coastline, killing more than 1,800 people and causing $100 billion in property damage. When the levees broke, low-lying New Orleans flooded. Initial emergency efforts, managed by the state of Louisiana, were ineffective; chaos reigned; and the nation was barraged with televised images of what looked like a third-world disaster. "The response was not only flawed ... but unacceptable," Bush later wrote. "[Katrina] eroded citizens' trust in their government. It exacerbated divisions in our society and politics. And it cast a cloud over my second term."

Top, during one of his many trips to the Gulf, Bush hugs hurricane victim Sandra Patterson, whose Biloxi, Mississippi, home was destroyed. **Bottom**, Federal Emergency Management Agency (FEMA) chief Michael Brown briefs the president and Secretary of Homeland Security Michael Chertoff. Brown would resign ten days later amid allegations of inexperience and incompetence. Democratic Louisiana Governor Kathleen Blanco, widely criticized for her ineffective leadership during the crisis, announced on March 20, 2007, that she would not seek a second term.

Facing page: Bush surveys the damage left by Hurricane Katrina as he flies over New Orleans in Air Force One. "When the pictures were released I realized I had made a serious mistake." Bush later wrote, "The photo of me hovering over the damage suggested I was detached from the suffering on the ground. That wasn't how I felt." During the seven weeks following the disaster, the president visited the Gulf Coast eight times.
Photographs by Win McNamee (top) and Jim Watson (bottom and facing page)

SUPREME COURT PICKS: During the summer of 2005, President Bush suddenly had two Supreme Court vacancies to fill—the first in eleven years. First, Reagan appointee Sandra Day O'Connor resigned to care for her ailing husband. Then Chief Justice William Rehnquist, a Nixon pick, died of thyroid cancer. Bush initially chose federal appellate judge John Roberts for O'Connor's seat. But when Rehnquist passed away, the president moved Roberts to the top spot and nominated White House Counsel Harriet Miers as associate justice. "I didn't like the idea of the Supreme Court having only one woman," Bush later wrote. When members of his own party criticized the choice, Miers withdrew and Bush tapped Third Circuit Court of Appeals Judge Samuel Alito of New Jersey, an experienced jurist with a dependably conservative record. **Left**, President Bush with Supreme Court Justices, **l–r**, John Paul Stevens, Ruth Bader Ginsburg, David Souter, Antonin Scalia, Chief Justice John Roberts, and retiring justice Sandra Day O'Connor. **Above**, the president introduces Judge Samuel Alito as his nominee to replace Justice O'Connor.
Photographs by Ken Heinen (left) and Luke Frazza (above)

If you want a friend in Washington, get a dog.

—ATTRIBUTED TO
PRESIDENT HARRY TRUMAN

▶ **A PRESIDENT'S BEST FRIEND:** The Bushes had three White House dogs: English springer spaniel Spotty Fetcher (1989–2004); Scottish terrier Barney (né Bernard), shown here snuggling with the president on the Oval Office couch; and second-term addition Miss Beazley, also a Scottie. With dogs, as with politics, the Bushes kept it in the family. Spotty, son of Millie, was born in the White House during the first President Bush's administration. Miss Beazley's dad was Barney's half-brother. Barney's mom belonged to George W. Bush's first Environmental Protection Agency administrator, Christine Todd Whitman.

Photograph by Eric Draper

▲ **MIDTERMS:** On election day in 2006, President Bush returns to the White House after casting his vote in Crawford, Texas. His thumbs-up proved overly optimistic. In the midterms, the Democrats gained control of the Senate for the first time since 2002 and the House for the first time since 1995.
Photograph by Chip Somodevilla

▶ **THE SURGE:** Most Americans saw the Republicans' 2006 midterm defeat as a referendum on Iraq, which over the course of three and a half years had devolved into a bloody, sectarian civil war. At the time, most Democrats and many Republicans—Senator John McCain was a notable exception—urged the president to withdraw troops from the war zone. But Bush, unwilling to accept failure in Iraq, took the opposite tack, announcing on January 10, 2007, a temporary "surge" of 20,000 additional troops to stabilize the country. To head this effort, Bush tapped General David Petraeus, an Iraq War veteran who had pacified the town of Mosul and overseen the publication of the Army's counterinsurgency manual. Despite widespread skepticism, Bush's surge worked. Over a period of years, violence receded to a point where troop levels could be cut. Bush's successor, Barack Obama, would move General Petraeus first to US Central Command and then to Afghanistan.
Photograph by Jason Reed

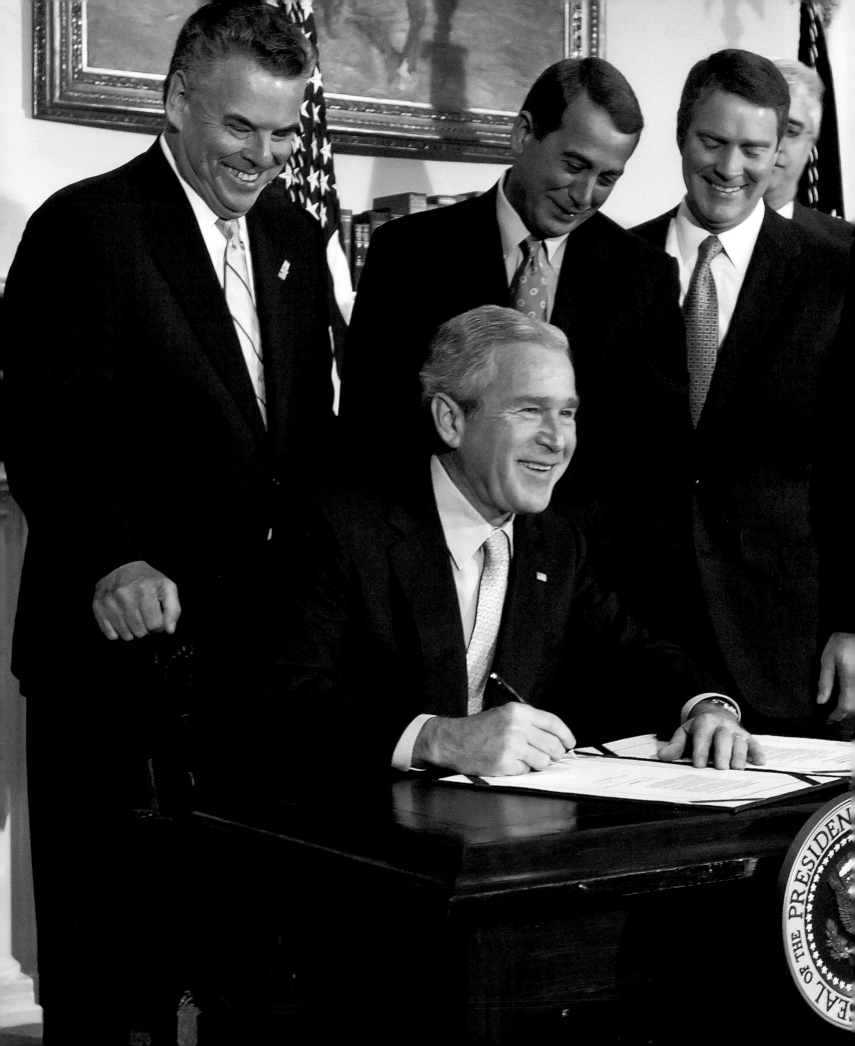

America's economy was a magnet for the poor and the hopeful. The longest and tallest fence in the world would not stop those determined to provide for their families.

—George W. Bush in
Decision Points, 2010

◄ **BORDER FENCE:** At the White House, President Bush signs the Secure Fence Act of 2006, authorizing a 700-mile barrier along the border between the United States and Mexico. Behind the president are, **l-r**, the bill's sponsor, Representative Peter King of New York; House Majority Leader John Boehner of Ohio; Senate Majority Leader Bill Frist of Tennessee; and Vice President Dick Cheney. At the time, the president said, "This bill will help protect the American people. This bill will make our borders more secure. It is an important step toward immigration reform." But he would later note that the border fence was, at best, a partial measure.
Photograph by Roger L. Wollenberg

BAILOUT: **Above**, in the Oval Office, President Bush signs the Emergency Economic Stabilization Act of 2008, more popularly known as the Wall Street bailout. When the US housing bubble burst in 2007—US home prices had risen nearly 90 percent since Bush took office, then dropped precipitously—borrowers defaulted on their mortgages, and large Wall Street firms, heavily invested in mortgage-backed securities, began to fail. Federal Reserve Chairman Ben Bernanke informed Bush that he faced the worst financial crisis since the Great Depression. Despite his philosophical commitment to free markets, Bush knew that only massive government intervention could forestall a worldwide economic meltdown. "As unfair as it was to use the American people's money to prevent a collapse for which they weren't responsible," wrote the president, "it would be even more unfair to do nothing and leave them to suffer the consequences." **Right**, President Bush walks with Treasury Secretary Henry Paulson. The bailout, signed by the president, gave Paulson a $700 billion line of credit—approximately 25 percent of the 2008 federal budget—to purchase "troubled" mortgage-backed assets. Paulson bought stock in troubled financial institutions instead.

Photographs by Brendan Smialowski

MY FRIEND AND MY PRESIDENT, GEORGE W. BUSH

By Donald L. Evans

Chairman, The George W. Bush Foundation

Former US Secretary of Commerce (2001–2005)

Two months after September 11, 2001, President George W. Bush hosted Russian president Vladimir Putin at the White House and Prairie Chapel Ranch in Crawford, Texas. In Washington, President Bush announced a reduction in America's nuclear arsenal—a decision that was matched by the Russians and helped put the Cold War even further behind us. Just as important as the formal meetings in Washington was the chance for President Bush to conduct personal diplomacy in Crawford. During dinner at the Bushes' ranch house, President Putin rose and gave a powerful toast. He remarked that during his presidency, he'd met with foreign leaders in capitals all around the world. But this was the first time a head of state had invited him into his home.

Putin's toast captured the warm, welcoming kindness of the entire Bush family. George W. Bush isn't imposing or intimidating. He is comforting and reassuring. He

◄ **HALO EFFECT:** The president speaks to the media during the first presidential news conference after his 2004 reelection. "Whatever the verdict on my presidency," Bush wrote in his 2010 autobiography, "I'm comfortable with the fact that I won't be around to hear it. That's a decision point only history will reach."

PHOTOGRAPH BY ALEX WONG

brings people—all people—into his space, onto his level. He treats paupers the same as presidents—with respect and good humor. As long as I've known him, his home has always been open to friends and guests. And his heart has always been open to his family and to his fellow citizens.

As long as I've known him, his home has always been open to friends and guests. And his heart has always been open to his family and to his fellow citizens.

The desire to serve others has always been in George W. Bush's blood. After he graduated from Yale, he volunteered to serve in the Texas Air National Guard. Before he went to Harvard Business School, he worked as a counselor at an inner-city youth program Houston. I witnessed his passion for public service firsthand when he ran for Congress in 1978 and lost. On election night, we stayed up late and watched the returns. As the night wore on, the outcome became increasingly clear. Rather than sulk, George W. Bush accepted the circumstances and started to think about other ways he might serve the Lone Star State. He was upbeat, positive, and optimistic. His capacity to accept defeat with grace, and his eagerness to find a new path to purpose, reminded me that this was a man devoid of ego, interested not in drawing the limelight, but in making a difference.

During that congressional campaign, I saw more than his desire to serve. I saw his talent for it. At a campaign rally in West Texas, the conversation covered local concerns: oil, gas, and cotton. Then a reporter threw a curveball in the form of an obscure foreign relations question about Turkey. I braced for a gaffe. Instead, Bush jumped all over the question. He articulated a visionary worldview and an understanding of geopolitics rarely seen in the Texas Permian Basin. His knowledge on such a wide range of issues and his innate ability to adapt to the unexpected were clear signs of a person who belonged in public office.

Another early indicator came in front of Laura Bush's mother's house in the summer of 1987. Midland summers were hot, and we were packing up the trucks to cool off for a weekend at my lake house with our families. I had a video camera and turned it on my friend. Acting like a mock news reporter, I asked, "Mr. Bush, what do you think of the state of affairs in the world today?" He didn't miss a beat. He dropped

In 2004, US Secretary of Commerce Donald Evans speaks to corporate executives, economists and academics at a White House Conference on the Economy. **Photograph by Alex Wong**

what he was doing, looked right into the lens of the camera, and surprised me with an impassioned agenda that started with education.

"I want to fix the education system in this country, beginning right here in Texas. I'm tired of a system that just shuffles kids through whether they learn or not. I have two young girls, and I owe it to them and to every child to make sure they have access to quality education."

It was a playful, spontaneous moment—and the coolers with Laura's freshly made cheese grits and luggage that we packed fell off the roof of our station wagon about five miles down the road—but the sentiment was real.

His desire to reform education was a motivating factor in George W. Bush's decision to run for office. It was so strong that he left a comfortable life in Dallas and a dream job with the Texas Rangers to run a race against Texas governor Ann Richards that his friends and even his mother said he couldn't win. He ran anyway, and his passion for education became a central plank in his campaign platforms for governor and later for the presidency. In office, he made good on that pre-campaign promise by bringing accountability and performance to schools, closing the achievement gap, and making sure no child got left behind. Of course, on September 11, 2001, everything changed. When terrorists attacked our country, President Bush vowed to do everything within his constitutional powers to protect our homeland. He did so in the face of withering criticism, and he overcame a slate of challenges few commanders in chief have ever faced.

His resolve came from an unshakeable inner strength. He found it in unconditional love from the parents he admired. He was grounded by his faith in God and comforted by the prayers of his fellow citizens.

His resolve came from an unshakable inner strength. He found it in unconditional love from the parents he admired. He was grounded by his faith in God and comforted by the prayers of his fellow citizens. He benefited from the perspective of his history major, and his optimistic vision for our future extended beyond the horizon. He had confidence in our country and a lifelong love for America. And he was raised with West Texas values and a set of principles that are inviolate.

President Bush's leadership was defined by a God-given strength of conviction and by those core principles: Freedom is a universal gift from God to every man, woman, and child on earth. Taxpayers can spend their own money better than the government can, and markets are the best way to allocate goods, resources, and services. All life is precious. Of those to whom much is given, much is required. And in everything, results matter. His belief in these core principles guided his decisions and gave him confidence in his purpose.

Because he worshipped not the power of the office, but a higher power, he led with clarity and poise. As he says, when you sit behind the Resolute Desk in the Oval Office where so many great leaders have preceded you, you realize that the office is

Office where so many great leaders have preceded you, you realize that the office is more important than the man who holds it. So he strengthened the institution of the presidency and brought integrity to the White House. He never compromised his principles for politics or popularity.

Above all, George W. Bush recognized that the single most important job of the president is to protect the people. So he kept us safe. And at the end of the day, he came home to Texas the same man who left eight years earlier. Sure, he was better traveled, and a little grayer, but he was the same. Through the photographs in these pages, I hope you get a sense of the kind, generous man who was honored to serve our country—the man I am honored to call my friend and my president, George W. Bush.

Midland, Texas
March 2011

HANDOVER: Left, on election day in 2008, President Bush, calling from the White House Treaty Room, congratulates Democratic president-elect Barack Obama, who decisively beat Republican standard-bearer John McCain. **Above**, six days later, Bush hosted Obama in the Oval Office, while Laura Bush gave incoming First Lady Michelle Obama a tour of the residence. The Obama camp characterized the visit as "warm and productive."
Photograph by Eric Draper

▶▶ **GOODBYE TO ALL OF THAT: Following pages**, After the inauguration of the forty-fourth president, number 43, George W. Bush, looks out over the US Capitol, still festooned in red, white, and blue, as his helicopter heads toward Andrews Air Force Base. At Andrews, George and Laura Bush boarded Air Force One, now designated Special Air Mission 28000, for the trip home to Midland, Texas. The next morning, "I was struck by the calm," Bush later wrote. "There was no CIA briefing to attend, no blue sheet from the Situation Room.... I would read the news and instinctively think about how we would have to respond. Then I remembered that decision was on someone else's desk."
Photograph by Eric Draper

REFERENCES & SOURCES

The quotations on pages 10, 13, 17, 40, 45, 49, 58, 69, 93, 131, 132 and 133 are from Barbara Bush, *A Memoir* (Scribner, 1993).

The quotations from George H. W. Bush's contemporaneous letters and diary entries on pages 19, 21, 22, 30, 31, 35, 38, 39, 40, 46, 57, 58, 61, 66, 75, 87, 88, 94, 96, 99, 100, 105, 107, 109, 110, 114, 115, 116, 118, 121, 122, 124, 131, 135 and 143 are from George Bush, *All the Best, My Life in Letters and Other Writings* (Scribner, 1999).

The quotations on pages 43, 63, 65, 138, 147, 154, 155, 167, 168, 173, 175, 178, 191, 194, 197, 200, 205, 209, 210, 213 and 219 are from George W. Bush, *Decision Points* (Crown, 2010).

The quotation on page 189 is from Laura Bush, *Spoken from the Heart* (Scribner, 2010).

Other books used in the preparation of this book include:

Nigel Hamilton, *American Caesars: Lives of the Presidents from Franklin D. Roosevelt to George W. Bush* (Yale University Press, 2010)

John Lindsay-Poland, *Emperors in the Jungle: The Hidden History of the U.S. in Panama* (Duke University Press, 2003)

Timothy Naftali, *George H. W. Bush: The American Presidents Series* (Times Books, 2007)

Karl Rove, *Courage and Consequence: My Life as a Conservative in the Fight* (Simon & Schuster, 2010)

Peter Schweizer and Rochelle Schweizer, *The Bushes: Portrait of a Dynasty* (Anchor, 2005)

Paul Thompson, *The Terror Timeline: Year by Year, Day by Day, Minute by Minute: A Comprehensive Chronicle of the Road to 9/11—and America's Response* (Harper Paperbacks, 2004)

Tom Wicker, *George Herbert Walker Bush, Penguin Lives Series* (Viking, 2004)

Printed sources used in the preparation of this book include:

The Associated Press
The Case-Schiller Index
The New York Times
Smithsonian
Time
Vanity Fair
The Washington Post

Web sites used in the preparation of this book, include:

www.americanrhetoric.com
www.bartleby.com
bushlibrary.tamu.edu
www.cbsnews.com
www.cnn.com
www.debates.org
www.fas.org
www.firstladies.org
www.foxnews.com
www.gallup.com
www.guardian.co.uk
www.history.navy.mil
www.millercenter.org
www.nga.gov
www.pbs.org
www.politico.com
www.politifact.com
www.wikipedia.org
www.womansday.com
www.wsj.com

PORTRAIT OF 41 AND 43: The first father and son presidents since 1829, photographed at Camp David by presidential photographer Eric Draper in April 2008.

CONTRIBUTORS

Text by David Elliot Cohen and Curt Sanburn

Foreword by Condoleezza Rice

Essay by Donald L. Evans

Designed by David Elliot Cohen

Page production and image processing by Premedia Systems, Inc.

Copyedited by Sherri Schultz

Proofread by Sharon Vonasch

THANKS TO:

The George Bush Presidential Library and Museum

Sarah Beaufait of Secretary Donald L. Evans' Office

Liesel Bogan of Prof. Condoleezza Rice's Office

Mary Finch and Bonnie Burlbaw of the National Archives and Records Administration

Michael Fragnito, Barbara Berger, Caroline Mann, Elizabeth Mihaltse, Laura Healy and Gillian Berman of Sterling Publishing

Jeremy Katz

Peter Robinson of the Hoover Institution

My wife, Laureen Seeger and our children—Kara, Will, Lucas, Angela and Grace

David Sherzer of President George W. Bush's Office

PHOTO SOURCES

AFP/Getty: 7, 145, 147, 148 (top), 149, 150, 151, 152 (bottom), 153 (top left), 154, 155 (2), 158, 162 (2), 163, 164, 165, 169, 170-171, 172, 175, 178 (top), 186, 195, 196, 197, 199 (bottom), 200 (bottom), 201, 203

Bettman Archive/Corbis: 4, 33

Corbis: 194, 211

Department of Defense/Getty: 177 (top)

Eric Draper Photography: 166-167, 168 (2), 173, 174, 177 (bottom), 178 (bottom), 188, 189, 191, 205, 219, 223

George Bush Presidential Library and Museum: 8 (2), 9, 10, 11, 12, 13, 14, 15, 16, 17 (2), 18, 19 (2), 20, 21 (2), 22, 23, 25, 26, 27 (2), 28 (top), 29, 30 (2), 34, 35 (2), 36, 37, 38-39 (4), 40, 41, 44, 45, 46, 47, 49, 50, 51, 54, 55, 56, 57 (2), 58 (2), 59, 60, 61 (2), 63, 64, 66 (2), 67, 68, 70-71, 73 (2), 86, 87 (2), 88, 89, 90, 91, 92, 93, 94-95, 96, 97, 98-99, 100, 101, 102-103 (4), 104, 105, 106-107, 108, 109, 110-111, 112, 113, 114, 115, 116, 117, 118-119 (4), 120, 121, 122, 123, 124, 125, 126, 127, 128, 130, 131, 132, 133, 134-135, 140

Getty Images: 69 (bottom), 138, 146, 148 (bottom), 158, 160-161 (2), 187, 188, 190, 192, 193, 197, 198 (top), 199 (top), 200 (top), 202, 206, 208, 210, 212, 215

Liaison/Getty: 52, 72, 136-137, 139 (bottom), 144, 153 (bottom), 156-157

New York Daily News/Getty: 152 (top), 198 (bottom)

Newsmakers/Getty: 3, 31, 42-43 (3), 48, 53, 62, 65, 153 (top right), 159

Reuters/Corbis: 207

Rykoff Collection/Corbis: 28 (bottom)

Saba/Corbis: 74, 129

Sygma/Corbis: 139 (top)

The White House/Getty: 176, 216, 218, 220-221

Time-Life Pictures/Getty: 24-25, 32, 69 (top), 141, 142-143